It's
GOOD
to Be
GRONK

It's GOOD *to Be* GRONK

ROB "GRONK" GRONKOWSKI

with *Jason Rosenhaus*

GALLERY BOOKS

JETER PUBLISHING

New York   London   Toronto   Sydney   New Delhi

JETER PUBLISHING

 Gallery Books/Jeter Publishing
An Imprint of Simon & Schuster, Inc.
1230 Avenue of the Americas
New York, NY 10020

First Gallery Books trade paperback edition June 2017

GALLERY BOOKS and colophon are registered trademarks of Simon & Schuster, Inc.

For information about special discounts for bulk purchases, please contact
Simon & Schuster Special Sales at 1-866-506-1949 or business@simonandschuster.com.

The Simon & Schuster Speakers Bureau can bring authors to your live event.
For more information or to book an event, contact the Simon & Schuster Speakers Bureau at
1-866-248-3049 or visit our website at www.simonspeakers.com.

Pages 1, 2, and 3: All photos courtesy of Diane Gronkowski Walters; *Page 4:* First two photos:
Courtesy of Author's Collection; third photo: Courtesy of Brent Coward; *Page 5:* First two
photos: Courtesy of Author's Collection; *Page 8:* First photo: Photoshoot with Martin Schoeller
for *ESPN the Magazine* courtesy of Stacey Pressman; second photo: Courtesy of Author's
Collection

Interior design by Jaime Putorti

Manufactured in the United States of America

10 9 8 7 6 5 4 3 2 1

Library of Congress Cataloging-in-Publication Data is available.

ISBN 978-1-4767-5500-7 (pbk)
ISBN 978-1-4767-5480-2 (hardcover)
ISBN 978-1-4767-5506-9 (ebook)

DEDICATIONS

Rob:

I would like to dedicate this book to my father, Gordy,

and my mom, Diane, who have both given everything

to make me and my four brothers happy and successful.

Jason:

To my dearest sweet little daughter, Aubrey,

you are the best of me and are becoming

more like your mother every day. I love you.

1

MEET THE GRONKS

From day one, all I ever wanted to do was have fun with my brothers. Whether that fun came from playing sports, joking around, dancing crazy, wrestling, or just being me, that was what made me happy. And now, twenty-something years later I refuse to let success, money, fame, beautiful women, or anyone or anything else change me. Why should I change? I'm a happy guy, I don't hurt anyone (except when I'm paid to do it on the football field), I work superhard, I don't break the law, and I'm all about working hard, playing hard, and being a good guy to the kids. What's wrong with that? Absolutely nothing, so I'm going to play ball, work out in the gym, hit my playbook, run on the track, party with my family, and do all of it Gronk-style!

That doesn't mean I'm going do things my way or not at all. That means I'm gonna do things the right way, the best way I can or not at all. That's how I was raised and that's who I am. There was no other way for me to be. I grew up in a house in Buffalo, New York, with four brothers. In that house, we had constant fun and action. Our idea of fun was beating the hell out of each other and laughing the whole time as we got our shots in. I had three older brothers and one younger brother and we did nothing but all-out brawl all day, every day. My poor mom, Diane, had no chance of handling all of us and my dad, Gordy, set two rules we all had to follow—no punching to the face, or to the balls. Anything other than that, and I mean anything, was fair game.

One afternoon my dad came home from work and walked into the kitchen to see what the ruckus was. My older brother Chris, who was fifteen at the time, had me, thirteen, pinned on my back. The loud thumping my dad heard was Chris grabbing fistfuls of my hair with both hands and smacking the top of my head back and forth into the linoleum kitchen floor. My dad, who is a big man himself, and had played college football, picked us both up with each arm and held us against the wall. "That's it! We're gonna settle this right now."

My dad was our idol; he was big, strong, tough, and smart. We all respected him and his two rules mostly because he was the only thing in the world we were afraid of. He was mean when he had to be, but always fair. After separating us, my dad brought us into the living room and cleared out the couch and other furniture so the center of the room was empty. He gave us both one of the big pillows on the couch and let us smash into each other full speed until we tired ourselves out. He called it zoom-zoom. From then on, whenever he had to break up a fight between us, we resolved it through zoom-zoom, where we banged into each other, over and over again like only kids can do, until we were both exhausted. We loved it!

Another time, when I was eight and Chris was ten, I caught him taking one of my Reese's Pieces packets from my Halloween candy bag. Back then, Halloween candy was like gold to us. We would spend the night running from house to house with huge pillowcases to grab and carry as much candy as we could. Whoever had the biggest bag with the most candy had the best night among all of us. It was a major competition in our household.

That year, I was particularly proud of my large bag of candy and guarded it like it was pirate treasure. When Chris took a Reese's Pieces packet from my bag, I went nuts. I grabbed one of my mini hockey sticks (it's about a foot long) and ran toward him and checked him as hard as I could. Before Chris could get up, I started whacking him with the stick. Chris fought his way up and ran after me. Chris was a lot bigger and more muscular than I was since he was stocky and older. Since I was smaller than my older brothers, my technique was to hit them with the best shot I could and then run off and try to escape.

After knocking Chris down, I sprinted toward the bathroom and tried to close the door behind me, but Chris was coming full speed. He put his shoulder into it and barreled through the door. I was caught off balance and the force of the door sent me flying backward. I hit the back of my head on the front of the hard bathtub and was knocked out cold.

When Chris saw I wasn't moving, he thought I was dead and he ran off into the living room in a panic, calling for our parents. While Chris was panicking in the living room, I woke up, grabbed my stick, and went right back at him. By the time my dad came downstairs, Chris got checked from behind and was knocked to the floor.

To understand us, you have to picture five boys growing up together in the same household in upstate New York. The oldest, Gord (not to be confused with our dad, Gordy), is the most outgoing, fun-loving, and partying guy of the group. Gord went on to play professional baseball and was a tall first baseman. Gord was six years older than me. Next came Danny, who was the biggest and best athlete around but was always responsible and mature for his age. Dan was four years older than me. Then came Chris, who was an intimidating, mean, and scary kid. Chris enjoyed inflicting pain on everyone who would bother him. Chris was two years older than me and I fought him the most. Then came Glenn, who we all call Goose. Goose is four years younger than me and he took a beating the same as everyone else.

To me, fighting my brothers was fun. The problem was that I was smaller than Gord, Dan, and Chris. These were really big guys who would all become professional athletes. Since I was younger and smaller, the only way to even the odds was to hit them with whatever I could find and then run like hell to escape. Most of the time I got away but when I didn't, I took my beating like a man.

One afternoon, my dad's brother, my uncle Glen, came over to visit us. I loved Uncle Glen. He was a fun uncle to talk with so I was pissed off when I saw Dan talking to him where I had been sitting five minutes earlier. I had just gone into the kitchen for a minute to get something to eat and when I came back Dan had taken my seat. When I saw Dan laughing it up with Uncle Glen, I was determined to get him. I didn't care that Dan had no idea he pissed me off and that it was unintentional. Once I had any reason to attack, any reason whatsoever, I was gonna take my best shot. So I snuck out of the kitchen behind Dan and with a full sprint toward the living room, tackled Dan all-out. I rammed my elbow right into the back of his ribs and got him good.

Dan had no clue what had happened but he knew the drill. He knew I didn't need much of a reason and got up instantly to chase me down. Dan was four years older than me and bigger, faster, and stronger than I was. To make things worse, Chris was there and saw what I did, so for the fun of it and because I deserved it, Chris helped Dan catch me, grab me, and hold me down. From there, Dan just pounded me in my thighs, punching me over and over again, giving me a brutal charley horse. That was their deal. Dan and Chris knew my dad would knock the hell out of them if they punched me in the face or balls, so they stayed within the rules and did their worst!

Whenever they could catch me, and that was most of the time, Chris would hold me down and Dan would savagely, without mercy, whale on me with his fists, elbows, and knees. The thing is, I always deserved it because I had always started it. And I always started it because after a while, my thighs, shoulders, arms, and stomach all toughened up and the blows didn't hurt anymore. So when I got caught and no matter how hard they punched, elbowed, and kneed me, I could take it and started laughing uncontrollably. It was so much fun to me to tackle them when they weren't looking and I liked it when they beat the hell out of me. There was just nothing they could do to stop me, so it was a nonstop cycle of brawling.

I don't know why I always started the trouble. Dan didn't deserve for me to tackle him and elbow him in the back of his ribs. He never bullied me or picked on me. But when I started it, he would do his best to finish it and make me pay for it.

Dan was a really good kid. He was the all-American guy you would want to marry your daughter. He was the biggest and best athlete wherever he went, did really well in school, and as I said, was very mature for his age. Chris, on the other hand, was not a really good kid. While wicked smart with his grades, Chris got my father's mean streak and took it to the next level. Chris enjoyed beating me up and dishing out pain. Whenever Dan gave me a charley horse it was only because I really pushed his buttons. I didn't need to push Chris's buttons; he was always ready to throw punches, elbows, and knees. He loved beating me up and I loved trying to get him back. I wasn't afraid. For whatever reason, I loved causing trouble and pissing people off, it was fun. Because Chris was closest to me in age, I always wanted to do what he was doing and whenever I couldn't, I would tackle him, elbow, knee him—whatever shots

I could get in, I took. And when Chris wasn't around, I would fight Dan even though he was twice my size and four years older.

Because they were bigger than me I had to use whatever I could get my hands on to help even the odds. My favorite weapon of choice was the Gronk family trumpet. At our elementary school, everyone had to play the trumpet in the fifth grade. It started with Gord, was passed down to Dan, then to Chris, then to me, and then to Goose. When Gord had it, it was shiny and in perfect condition. By the time I got it, that thing looked like it had been run over by a car. It had dents and scratches on it everywhere. I don't know how the thing still worked when Goose got it.

The dents and scratches are from when I used to come after Dan with it. I couldn't help but be angry when Dan would tease me about anything. If we just played a game downstairs in the basement or in the backyard and I lost, any type of bragging on their part or criticism of my game would set me off. If I won, I would start teasing them over and over again until they couldn't take it anymore, and things would escalate pretty quickly and get out of hand, Ron Burgundy–style.

I remember Dan was babysitting at home one night and he had had enough of my smart-aleck remarks and told me to go upstairs to my room. He warned me not to come back downstairs. I was angry so I went right upstairs, into his room, grabbed the trumpet out of the case, and came downstairs yelling at him, holding it over my head. For once I was doing the chasing and Dan was doing the running. I couldn't catch him so I threw it at him and missed, which I probably did intentionally. He was super-mad and I knew he would beat the hell out of me, but I didn't care. I wasn't afraid. Over the years, I came at him a lot with that trumpet but I never really got him full-contact with it.

The trumpet wasn't the only thing I threw. One time I threw a fork at Dan. I can't even remember why, but I missed him anyway. The problem was I hit the babysitter with it and it stuck into her hand. The poor lady had had no idea what she signed up for when she had to pull the fork out of her hand. She obviously didn't come back.

No matter what I threw at Sweet Pete, he always came back. Sweet Pete was Dan's best friend in high school. Dan played quarterback and his left tackle was Pete DeAngelo. He lived down the block and was always over. Back then, "sweet" meant cool, so it was a compliment, and Pete had a big head as one of the cool kids. When Sweet Pete would come over, we would play some type of mini-hockey-stick game downstairs in the basement. More important than winning and scoring goals was seeing who could check who the hardest into the concrete foundation wall.

Now, Sweet Pete was 6'1" and 215, which was pretty big for high school. Since I was four years younger than Sweet Pete, he was still stronger and bigger than I was, but I didn't care.

Whatever game they were playing, I wanted to play. Whatever they were doing, I wanted to do. And no matter what, by the end of the day, Pete and I would always go at it. He loved beating me up. If I didn't start with him, he would start with me. Whenever he and I were in the house together, there was going to be a battle.

I would tease Pete all the time and tell him he wasn't sweet (meaning he was not cool). I would say that and whatever else aggravated him over and over again until he and Dan couldn't take it anymore and they came after me. They would tackle me, hold me down, and charley-horse my thighs and shoulders, but I didn't feel any pain. I couldn't help but laugh uncontrollably the whole time. They beat the hell out of me but I loved it.

There aren't too many people who can walk around and say they beat the hell out of Rob Gronkowski all the time, but Sweet Pete can. But now the tables have obviously turned and things have changed. Sweet Pete still likes to brag to everyone that he toughened me up and made me the man I am today, etc. . . . And it finally caught up to him at Dan's bachelor party in Las Vegas in the summer of 2011.

That crazy weekend, we went to Vegas for Dan's bachelor party and stayed at the Hard Rock Hotel. Dan had this monster suite where me, Gord, Dan, Chris, Goose, and Sweet Pete were staying. The suite had a huge couch on it. After we had one drink too many, Sweet Pete, who is now in shape at 6′1″ and 250 pounds, started talking trash that he could still take me. He played center on the Ithaca College football team in New York and said he could knock me on my butt.

He was loud and animated, talking trash to me. He actually climbed up on the couch and got into a three-point stance and challenged me to do the same opposite him and see who could knock who off the couch.

Now, I hadn't wrestled with Pete since I was in the eighth

grade, so it had been over ten years since we last matched up, but I had been waiting a long time to get even with him. He must have checked me like a thousand times into that concrete wall as hard as he could and celebrated each time like he had just won the Stanley Cup. So in Vegas I couldn't resist and jumped at the chance.

Next thing I know, Sweet Pete dove low and went all-out, knocking me off balance, and I fell off the couch. He jumped up and cheered once again like he did in the old days. I didn't like losing at all so I immediately said, "Two out of three, let's go!"

He was still talking smack but as he lined up, I looked right into him and he knew I was going to bring it. To his credit, he didn't back down and came after me. This time I took him seriously and got the jump on him. I exploded into him and knocked him straight back and up in the air. He somehow flipped over and landed on his face. He didn't move for a second and then he picked his face up and the side of it was red. Sweet Pete got a big black eye and spent the whole weekend walking around with it. The thing took forever to heal and he brought it back to work with him for a week. I'm not going to lie, I don't feel bad about it at all. I love it! A little payback.

I guess some things don't change. I'm still the same as I was when I was kid. I remember one time we went on a family vacation to visit our uncle, who thought it would be a good idea to take Chris and me out on his sailboat. About twenty minutes into the journey I whacked Chris over the head with the big scoop fishnet on the boat. I obviously ruined the net but the boat managed to stay afloat until our uncle could get the boat turned around and safely back to shore. We were never taken on that boat again. My dad canceled the trip as punishment and took us home, but stuff like that was always happening where I would start trouble. I couldn't help myself; it was fun for me to play sports and fight with my brothers. That's all I did growing up.

The way things worked around the house, is that the younger brother would fight the next-older brother. Dan fought Gord. Chris fought Dan. I fought Chris and Goose did his best to fight me. The youngest was Goose, who was a tough little guy from day one, always trying to hang with us, but he was four years younger. Since there was that age difference, I was a lot bigger than Goose, but I didn't care. I treated him with the same respect as all of my other brothers and beat him up, too. I didn't care who it was: if I got angry, I was going to attack. Unless of course it was my dad.

My dad was a real patriarch, a man's man that every son could look up to. He played college football at Syracuse and was a big, nasty, tough offensive lineman. My dad had NFL potential but too many injuries ruined his chances. Back then in the 1970s, the surgeries weren't anything like they are today, where you have a fighting chance to come back better than ever. Though even today, you have to be lucky. My dad wasn't lucky with football, no matter how tough he was or how hard he tried; his future was not in the NFL. But he used those traits he learned from football in becoming a big-time businessman.

When sports were over, he didn't feel sorry for himself. If he couldn't make a living playing sports, he'd go out and make an even better one selling sports equipment. My dad started his own business with his brother and they sold weight-training and fitness equipment. He was resilient and never let the bad breaks break him. I wish he could have known back then when he was heart-broken over the injuries and saw his career end in college that he would go on to raise three sons who would play in the NFL.

The thing about my dad is that when the adversity came, he responded with mental toughness and hard work. A smart busi-nessman, he started one store and turned it into G&G Fitness Equipment, a chain of specialty fitness equipment stores in the Northeast. As busy as my dad was, he always made the time to be there for us. He coached us, he trained us, and most important, he instilled a good-spirited sense of competition between us. Rather than be jealous of each other or hate on one another, we all rooted for each other and pushed each other to break the record and set a new bar. My dad made sure we wouldn't turn out to be a bunch of knuckleheads who got into trouble. While some would look at us and think we were dumb jocks clowning around, all of us did well in school, went to college, and stayed clear of trouble. And while some of those same people might think that it is a miracle we didn't get thrown in jail, I know better because it wasn't by luck or coincidence. My dad drew a clear line and taught us well not to cross it, no matter what.

What I realize now is that there are so many other kids born with the genetics to play in the NFL and to be the best. The part that separates those super-gifted athletes who make it to the NFL and those who don't is knowing when to stop, knowing where that line is. My brothers and I go out to have fun, but we know when and where to stop. We are proof that you can go out and have a good time without doing drugs and getting into trouble. We are proof that you can play hard to the whistle and then stop before drawing a penalty. We are proof that you can be the biggest, baddest dude on the block without breaking the law or hurting someone.

It's not enough just to have the genetics to play in the NFL; you have to have the guidance growing up to do well in school and in athletics. My dad kept us out of trouble in the neighborhood by keeping us in trouble in the house. My mom somehow had the patience to deal with us wrecking the house every day. They put up with us constantly going at it and yet they still laid down the law. The rule (besides the one about no punches to the face or nuts) was that we were not to fight other kids (except to defend ourselves), because my parents didn't want us to get sued or arrested. Avoiding getting into fights with other kids wasn't a problem for us. The thing is, we were all big, and the more important point was that we had brothers. If you fought one of us, you had to fight all of us. So I never got into any street fights throughout high school, except for when I went to visit Dan and Chris at their college, but I will get into that a little later, I promise.

I didn't need to get into street fights because I was always getting into it at my house. Gord, six years older than me, had this one friend in high school who was a good wrestler. He would beat Gord and whenever I saw them wrestling, I would jump on the pile and do everything I could to hurt the guy and help Gord. The wrestler would get real angry and try to choke me out. The guy was six years older than me and although I was always really big for my age, he was still twice my size.

I also got another type of training at my house. I learned to have fun but not overdo it, or else you would pass out. Anytime one of our friends drank too much and passed out at the house, they got the Magic Marker treatment. I remember one night Sweet Pete drank too much and fell out. We were all pretty good artists. When Pete woke up, he walked downstairs and into the kitchen to have some cereal. My dad was in the kitchen eating his breakfast and looked up at him. We were all watching my dad very closely to see his reaction. My dad looked at him briefly with a straight poker face, said good morning, and then got up and walked upstairs, where we were waiting. As soon as my dad turned the corner, he couldn't hold it in anymore and laughed as quietly as he could.

What my dad was laughing about was that Sweet Pete had come downstairs with a huge penis drawn on both sides of his face. On his forehead it said, "I love d—k!" My dad had seen this before on the neighborhood kids who drank too much and slept over. He figured it would teach them a lesson not to overdo it. So nobody said anything to Sweet Pete until his dad came to pick him up.

So I was trained every day to play hard and have fun within the rules. That's how I grew up. Look at it this way: I had two older brothers who would go on to play in the NFL. I was always trying to beat them at whatever sports and games we could play at our house. Whenever I got angry, which was every time I lost, I would jump on whoever pissed me off and try to make him regret it. This kind of training all day, every day, year after year, trained me to be tough, athletic, and physical. Instead of being afraid to get hit, I couldn't wait to be the one to do the hitting. I was used to playing sports against my monster older brothers and their friends. When I got to play football against kids my age, I was twice their size and just destroyed them—it was super-fun! The other guy was always afraid, not me! It was this type of Spartan training with my older brothers that made me the Gronk!

2

BECOMING THE GRONK

My freshman year at Williamsville North High School I was very tall but not a dominant athlete. I was close to 6′5″ but thin at 210 pounds. The best way to describe it is that I didn't have my feet under me. I didn't feel powerful, quick, or fast. I wasn't coordinated like I wanted to be. I was playing on the junior varsity squad with other kids my age or younger, so I was the biggest kid around, but I was just the tallest, not the best. My goal was to keep working hard to get on the varsity squad at some point during my freshman year.

I was playing on both sides of the ball: defensive end, where I would try to sack the quarterback, and tight end—my natural position. Again, I was really lanky and tall but I didn't feel explosive or muscular. I was better on defense than I was offense. On defense, I could just run around the offensive line and try to get to the quarterback or, if it was a running play, just try to tackle the running back. I had really long arms compared to the other kids, and that helped me grab the guy and bring him down. On offense, it was harder for me to get separation, have good footing, keep my balance, have strong body positioning, fight for the ball, and catch it. I was good but not great and it really bothered me.

My brother Dan was off to the University of Maryland as a freshman and was now playing tight end there. He was a legend (in my mind) at our high school as the quarterback the year before. It was special to go from high school to Division 1 college football at Maryland. Dan had been a beast at high school and the same was expected of me, since I was his height.

My other brother Chris, a junior on the varsity team, was not as tall as us—he was 6'2"—but he was a killer. He played full-back and linebacker, the two most physical positions on the field. Chris was superstrong and played with a real mean streak. No one wanted to get in his way. Whether he was at linebacker or fullback, all he wanted to do was hit you so hard, you would quit. He was more interested in making the big hit than he was in scoring touch-downs or anything else. He lived for the big hit. I really looked up to Chris and it made me want to play that same way. I loved mak-ing tackles—that was pretty much what I was best at—but I wasn't able to hit really hard yet. I was frustrated but not down. I was con-fident that I would get strong enough to be a hard hitter like Chris.

I wanted to play with Chris against the bigger, better players on the varsity team. It seemed when we were growing up that I was always getting on Chris's nerves and sometimes he hated me, but now we were best friends; we were the Gronkowski brothers—something special to all of us. It meant everything to me to get upped to the varsity team with Chris and be a part of what I viewed as the ultimate action, where the big dogs were.

On the last week of the season, I finally got my chance. My coach, Mike Mammoliti, who we all called Coach Mammo, brought me up to play one game, the last game, on the varsity team. I wasn't supposed to get on the field; it was supposed to be an introduction to help me get ready for next year. Toward the end of the game, the coach put me in on kickoff coverage. When Coach Mammo came and told me to go in, I was so jacked up. I had so much energy, I couldn't wait to start running. I wasn't nervous. I wasn't scared. I was hyped up and wanted to make the play—just like my brothers would do.

When the kicker ran toward the ball and kicked it in the air, I ran with everything I had. I ran through the blocker and slammed into the returner, making the tackle. I jumped up screaming with excitement. I finally made that big hit and at the best time!

You see, it wasn't just about making a tackle. It wasn't just about a hard hit. It was about a freshman playing with the sophomores, juniors, and seniors. That one play was huge for me because it gave me the confidence to believe in myself, to believe that I could play high school football like Dan and Chris had done. The minute I stood up after making the play, I believed I could compete at the next level up. I would never doubt my athletic ability again. From that moment on, I always had the confidence that I could reach my goal. I had no idea at the time that I would become an NFL player, but I knew I could play varsity high school football and from there I became a young man on a mission.

My first goal was to gain muscle, to get stronger, faster, and more coordinated, and get my feet under me, so to speak. That summer after my freshman season, my coach told me to get ready for varsity and I did everything I could think of to do that. Chris and I would eat, eat, and eat some more. Whenever we saw food, Chris and I would say to each other, "Gain-weight program . . . got to eat!" And we ate everything in sight.

My mom was awesome in that she was constantly cooking, shopping, and making sure there was always something good to eat. At the time I didn't appreciate it, but it was my mom who made sure we hit the books and were good students. Dan and Chris were book smart and did very well in school. I, on the other hand, didn't have a lot of patience for school, but my mom really made me sit down and do my work, or else Dad would hear about it and there would be no more football for me. I don't know how she had the patience to deal with me because I loved driving her crazy with my shenanigans, but she was relentless, and never let me fail.

It bothers me that I wasn't nicer to her growing up. I didn't mean to be such a little smart-aleck or troublemaker; it was just my personality to push people. By that summer, though, I really appreciated her and tried harder to be a better son because she deserved it. Still, every now and again . . . I was up to my usual smart-aleck comments that irked her. I'm always gonna be me, crack a joke, laugh, be funny, not take life too seriously. I hate when she says I was the hardest one out of all of us growing up; it makes me feel bad. It makes me try harder to be a good son now.

Thanks to my mom's cooking, I was able to eat food around the clock and stuff my face that summer. I trained with Chris every day, lifting weights, doing push-ups, pull-ups, sit-ups, and whatever other exercise we could get into. Since my dad was in the fitness equipment business, he had the best fitness equipment available for us in our basement. My dad worked out with us and saw to it that we were lifting with the proper technique and doing it the right way.

Chris wanted to gain five pounds and I wanted to gain as much as I could. That summer, Chris put on his five pounds that he wanted and I put on fifteen pounds of muscle. I went from 210 to 225 pounds and it made a huge difference. With that added muscle, I got my feet under me and felt explosive, powerful, and fast. That combination made me feel unstoppable. When I came back from the summer and started my sophomore year, I was dominating people on both sides of the ball. At 6'5" and 225 pounds, I was the best athlete on the field and there wasn't anyone close.

After catching so many passes from Dan and Chris in the backyard, and working on catching passes all summer long, I was becoming a true tight end who could block, run, catch, and score. I have to admit, it was totally awesome to be bigger, stronger, and faster than everybody else. It was just so much fun for me to play football. I couldn't wait to practice and I couldn't wait to play in the games. I knew that in order for me to play every down possible, I would have to know that playbook inside and out. Coming from a football family where my dad and older brothers all played the game, knowing the playbook inside and out was easy for me. I may not have been book smart but I was football smart and Coach Mammo respected that about me. As much as I like clowning around, I was always serious when it came to paying attention at practice and knowing my assignments. Coach Mammo trained me to realize that if I wanted to play and be the focal point of the offense and defense, I had to know them; in fact I made sure I knew my plays better than anyone. Coach Mammo made me understand how important it was to take the mental aspect of the game seriously. Everything else was about having fun.

It was because I knew my plays and assignments that I was able to get away with joking around so much in practice to keep everything fun. My first game that sophomore season set the tone for the rest of the year. We were playing at home and I was playing right defensive end on defense as well as tight end on offense. They started the game off with a run away from my side. The quarterback faked like he was going to run toward me and then pitched it the other way right before I was going to hit him. I ran into the backfield, right past the quarterback, ran the guy down from behind, and dove on his back to bring him down. I had so much momentum that we tumbled into the players and coaches on the sideline. From the moment I came around the corner from behind and had my sights on him, I couldn't help but laugh the way I laughed when my brothers used to punch me in the thigh. It was just so much fun that I was laughing the whole time. I immediately got up from the tackle and ran back to the huddle. My coach was right there when I jumped up from the tackle and I told him, "Okay, time to have some fun."

Nothing was more fun to me than making that superhard hit that would make our whole team jump up and start cheering and yelling like wild men. I love getting hyped up and there was nothing like making that big hit to get everyone fired up! Chris was awesome at it and he made me want to excel at it, too.

The best part of my sophomore year was playing next to Chris, being on the same team, and taking on everyone else. My favorite play that sophomore year was not one where I scored a touchdown or made a big tackle. It came in a game where Chris and I were on offense. Chris was at fullback, and he kept going at it with an opposing linebacker who had a really big, obnoxious mouth. Every play they would smash into each other and that guy wouldn't shut up. Chris was getting the best of the guy, and it only made the linebacker talk even more trash.

On one play, Chris caught a short screen pass behind the line of scrimmage and that linebacker started yelling as he raced toward Chris to tackle him. As the guy was running full speed, screaming at the top of his lungs to try to intimidate Chris, I turned and made a beeline straight for him. In what's called a crack-back block, I came at him from the side and ear-holed him, knocking him off his feet. I leveled the guy, sent him flying on his back, and knocked the wind out of him. My whole team went wild and cheered. I basked in the glory! I didn't talk smack back then, but we won that game and from then on, I knew I could be like Dan and play college football.

The summer before my junior year, I was sad to see Chris leave to go off to college, but I was happy for him to go to Maryland and play with Dan. Still on the gain-weight program, I added ten more pounds of rock-solid muscle that summer. I went from 225 pounds to 235 pounds. I was now ready to take it to a whole new level.

That junior year, my opponents had to cheat and team up against me to stop me. No one could block me at defensive end or cover me at tight end one-on-one. I was taller, faster, bigger, stronger, quicker, and more explosive than anyone else. It was such a mismatch that it got frustrating, because the referees would let the other team get away with everything and I got away with nothing. The other guys would cheap-shot me, tackle me when they were only supposed to block me, and the refs didn't do anything about it. I got angry and would make my opponents regret it. I got even by pancaking them (knocking them on their back) so badly the refs would throw a flag just because it was so one-sided. When players would hold me, I would throw them five yards downfield and the ref would penalize me, not them. I wanted to complain or talk trash back but I was too tired because I was out of breath having to play every down—offense, defense, and special teams.

It was my junior year that I was truly dominant versus the other high school kids. My favorite game my junior year at Williamsville North High was when we played against Lockport High School and needed the win to get to the playoffs. That game, I scored a touchdown on a 48-yard fumble return, sacked the quarterback for a safety, and caught a touchdown pass. Although we missed the extra point, we won 15–0 off the 15 points I scored. After the game, Lockport's coach had seen enough of me, Chris, and Dan. He asked Coach Mammo, "Is this kid the last of Gronkowskis? I'm getting tired of coaching against them." Coach Mammo told him, "Nope, there's one more coming." True enough, four years later, Goose played against them and made an awesome leaping catch in the end zone to win the game. I was super-proud of him.

After that season, the college scholarship offers came in. I spent that summer putting on even more weight, adding ten pounds to go from 235 to 245 pounds.

It was that summer going into my senior year that I realized I could play in the National Football League. I looked up what the nation's top collegiate tight ends' performance numbers were at the NFL Combine and saw that I was bigger, faster, and stronger than the college guys being drafted into the NFL. I knew that if I kept working, stayed out of trouble and got good grades, and most of all, stayed healthy, I would have a real chance to be an NFL player.

I was really proud of the way I played my junior year because my dad and brothers were impressed. They knew how well I did and they were rooting for me. With Chris and Dan both at Maryland, I went to visit them.

I was beyond excited to go to a college bar. At 6′6″, 245 pounds, no one knew I was still in high school. I had never gone to a party outside the Buffalo area, so for me to go to a party with Dan and Chris at Maryland was the coolest thing in the world. I had really missed my brothers, so to hang out with them was a huge thrill.

We started off that Saturday going to a Maryland game. I was on the sideline being recruited to go there for school. Dan was in his fourth year as a redshirt junior and Chris was in his second year there. The best play of the game to me was on a kickoff return where Chris was blocking for the return man and absolutely destroyed a guy with a block that sent the defender flying. That was Chris's specialty—blowing people up.

After the big win, I went out to the big hangout bar with Dan, Chris, and a bunch of their teammates. As soon as we walked into the bar, the song "Jump Around" came on, and I was so fired up I just instinctively started jumping up and down as high as I could. My head actually hit the chandelier and although it hurt a little, I thought it was funny and so did everyone else, so I kept jumping. Here I was with a drink in each hand jumping up and down like a madman, getting everyone soaked with beer and accidentally hitting Dan's roommate, Kyle Sappington, in the head with a bottle. Kyle was a freshman and really looked up to Dan as a leader on and off the field since Dan was such a smart and mature guy. Dan had graduated in only three years and was already pursuing his master's degree. Kyle couldn't believe I was his brother, and like everyone else there, he let me be me without causing a problem. The place was a football player hangout bar so the guys there were all friendly. Everyone looked at me like I was crazy but once Dan and Chris started jumping around, they did too. Before long, the whole place was jumping around and everyone got in on the fun.

The only time the players at the bar didn't follow our lead was when we sat down and ate pizza. The way we Gronks eat pizza is to have blue cheese dressing on our pizza. Hey—we're from Buffalo and that's how we did it then and still do it now.

I came home idolizing my older brothers. There was something about each one that I wanted to be like. I love how Gord is always positive, having fun and enjoying himself. I love how Dan is always successful at what he does, he's like Mr. Perfect at everything and is a leader. Chris is a cross between the two but is really mean, nasty, and tough. Along with my dad, they were my role models, I looked up to them and I couldn't wait to go to college and be like them. But before I could go to college and play NCAA football, I had to prove to the college teams that I was the real deal.

As luck would have it, we moved in my senior year to Pittsburgh, where I could play at Woodland Hills High School—the best school for football in the state. The athletes there were as good as any high school players in the country. This was my opportunity to compete with the best. Back home, I didn't know if I was that good because of a lack of competition, where I was just so much bigger than everyone else, or if I was truly one of the best high school football players in the country. Playing at Pittsburgh would tell me everything I wanted to know about myself as a football player.

I was used to playing on a high school football team with twenty-five guys on the roster who would play both offense and defense. At Woodland Hills, the roster was a hundred players, of which only a small handful would play offense and defense; everybody else would focus on trying to get playing time at one position. It would also be very different because back in Buffalo I would get five or six catches a game and had been the focal point of the offense as a playmaking tight end.

My Pittsburgh coach, George Novack, told me that they would be running the ball almost every play and that I would probably average one catch per game. This was a whole new challenge for me. I was used to just going up against the smaller, less athletic kids from Buffalo. I would be blocking every play as a tight end and playing defensive end against teams that primarily run the ball. This would be about battling in the trenches. Now I was going to go up against the strongest, most talented, most athletic players in the state. This was all new to me, as now I would be the minority white boy and everybody was going to come at me to see if I was tough enough to compete.

It's not enough to be big. You have to be tough and physical because in the trenches, the low man wins. If you block high and your opponent is lower than you, he will be able to use his legs to drive you backward. It's all about getting low, getting your hands on your opponent, and knocking him off balance and driving him backward.

I hadn't even been tested before against someone superstrong until that season. That first game could have been intimidating and scary but I worked so hard in practice, I was confident I could hold my own. Practice got me game ready.

I remember we were playing our school's rival team, and they had a defensive end matched up against me who was supposed to be a monster. He was big too, and talked more trash to me than anyone I had ever gone up against. He was calling me a soft white boy, he was telling me I was overrated, that I was nothing, that I was garbage, that I was all hype, and that he was going to kick my butt on every play.

I wasn't intimidated. I was feeling a little bit of everything but most of all it made me amped up to prove it wasn't true. I had spent my whole life growing up playing against my huge older brothers, so no one was going to scare me. So I pancaked him, put him on his back, and then when he tried to get up, I threw him down again. I beat him into the ground, play after play, until the whistle blew. My teammates loved it and it was more fun to me than catching touchdowns. I didn't talk trash because I was too tired from playing both offense and defense.

It seemed like I played every down because it was so exhausting to go all-out and give it my best effort every play. That season was all about blocking and wrestling linemen down to the ground. I learned a great deal about using my hands and blocking technique. And even though I was going up against the best in the state, it was the same old story where I beat my opponent down and they had to cheat and hold me and double-team me.

That whole season I had only eight catches, but five of them were for touchdowns. And even though I didn't get much action as a receiving tight end like I would have in Buffalo, all that blocking helped me tremendously to be a complete tight end, where blocking is a huge part of my game. It just seemed like I was wrestling every play on offense, and on defense as a defensive end stuffing the run if they tried to run to my side. My senior year was all about taking on the best athletes in the state and being more physical and tough. That year I became just as good a blocker as I was anything else.

As well as I played at defensive end, I always wanted to be a tight end. And even though I got only one pass a game, I made it count. I remember this one play where I lined up wide toward the sideline like a wide receiver. Since I was out wide, I was being covered by a cornerback who was superfast. When the ball was snapped, I gave him a quick stutter step, which made him freeze for a split second, and then I exploded off the line and ran downfield but inside toward the center of the field. The cornerback thought it was a post route where the receiver runs deep toward the middle of the end zone. He turned on the jets and sprinted toward the inside to try to stay with me, but as soon as he hit full stride and was totally committed to run inside, I made a fast break outside toward the corner of the end zone. The route was actually a fade route where you try to sell the defender that you are running a post inside and once he buys it, you fake him out and sprint outside. The quarterback made a perfect throw; I jumped up high, caught the ball, and came down with the 25-yard touchdown. It looked like an NFL play. Even though I was being used as a blocking tight end 99 percent of the time, that play reassured me that my receiving skills were still big-time.

Although my receiving stats weren't significant, I knew I had accomplished my goal of getting full scholarship offers to go to college. Sixty schools sent me scholarship offers. I now had the biggest choice of my life in front of me—where to go to college and play Division 1 football.

3

WILDCATS

My senior year in high school was challenging but awesome on so many different levels. With football, it was the best feeling in the world to know that I was one of the most talented high school football players in the country, and I believed that if I stayed healthy, I could one day play in the NFL. Second, moving to Pittsburgh my senior year was like going away to college. I had left all of my friends back in Buffalo, and my older brothers were out of town. So I got a head start experiencing what it was like to leave home and get adjusted. Still, I felt a little homesick, so I decided to visit Danny and Chris again at Maryland. I had so much fun the last time I was on their campus, I couldn't wait to go again.

It was awesome to walk around a college campus. I knew

I would be making my decision on which college program I would be going to and visiting them was a great start. I went to a Maryland game to root on the Terrapins and hung out with all the guys again after the game. I didn't realize how much I loved being around my brothers until I was with Dan and Chris. I just got hyped being around them and it fired me up. I had so much energy and wanted to have fun. Chris and I went to a bar on campus and got the night started as usual by dancing around, talking to girls, and having a few beers. Now, the dancing we do is like extreme dancing, where you are moving a hundred miles per hour and just getting crazy. It's a real workout. After a while, we decided to leave the bar and walk to a different party.

As Chris and I were walking up a small hill on a sidewalk, a group of six guys were walking toward us on the sidewalk. They were part of a fraternity, as most guys on that campus were. As they walked by us, they didn't want to move out of the way and neither did we.

The sidewalk was crowded and the guy didn't want to step around me and walk on the grass, so he bumped his shoulder into mine. After he bumped me, I kept walking but he turned around and obnoxiously said, "What the f—k! —hole!"

Chris and I both stopped at the same time, looked at each other, and smiled, nodding at each other because we knew what was going to happen next.

"Shut up!" I yelled back at the guy, and everybody was talking trash and threatening to fight. I was thinking this was awesome!

We were outnumbered six to two but I had my brother with

me and Chris was a badass fighter. They started it, they were looking for a fight, and at that time, fighting to me was fun. Chris wasn't going to let that jerk talk that way to his younger brother. Chris got right in that guy's face and all eight of us were talking smack. One of them threw the first punch at Chris and it was on.

Before anyone else could move, Chris punched the guy who tried to hit him and the guy staggered backward, holding his face. My eyes lit up and to me it was like playing football or dancing, it just came natural to me and with my long reach, I jabbed with my left and threw a good punch with my right to deck the guy in front of me.

I didn't see it, but somebody did a leaping kick from behind into my back and it knocked me down the hill about eight feet. I looked up to check on Chris and saw him throw the guy who had kicked me down the hill. That guy got up right near me and I punched him back down, then I ran up the hill to help Chris.

Chris didn't need my help. He was punching, grabbing guys, kneeing them, and throwing them off him. In a split second I was back up to the sidewalk and threw a haymaker right at a guy coming for Chris. It was like we were playing king of the hill, throwing everybody down. It didn't take long for them to want no further part of getting their butts kicked, so they kind of froze and Chris grabbed me to get out of there before the cops or more of their friends showed up.

We ran back to Chris's apartment and when we got there, we found out the cops had arrested some of the other guys. We weren't marked up but the other guys had been. Chris's roommate was there in the apartment and said there had been some big fight. Chris and I were dying laughing that we had gotten away from the cops and those idiots didn't. We couldn't help ourselves and told him it had been us. Dan walked in and knew right away it was us and just started laughing, too. I never had more fun in my life!

When I got back to Pittsburgh, it was time to take some college visits with my dad and figure out where I was going to go to school. I visited Syracuse because my dad went there and I liked it. I visited Ohio State because they were a national championship–caliber football program and was super-impressed. I visited Clemson and absolutely loved their game-day atmosphere at Death Valley. I considered Maryland but Chris wasn't happy there and was looking to transfer.

Chris and I were very interested in going to the same school together and when Chris was coming out of college, I went with him when he visited the University of Arizona. My dad had a close friend who was a big-time Arizona alumnus, Donnie Salum (pronounced like "Salem"). Donnie was like an uncle to us. He was a very successful fitness equipment distributor for the West Coast, like my dad on the East Coast. They had known each other a long time and became close friends over the years. Since Donnie had played at Arizona in the late 1980s, Donnie stayed close to the program and was a big shot there. Since both of our families had taken trips together over the years, I had become friendly with Donnie's nephew, Justin, who was my age. Justin was a good running back and wide receiver and was going to the University of Arizona on scholarship as well. Chris and I loved the weather, the fun atmosphere, and the football coaches. I was confident that regardless of whether I went to Ohio State, Clemson, or Arizona, if I played well enough, I could get to the NFL.

With Chris wanting to go to Arizona, with Justin going there, and with our oldest brother, Gord, playing minor league professional baseball there, it seemed like a dream situation for me to go to Arizona. So Chris and I both made the decision to go to Arizona and become Arizona Wildcats!

My dad purchased a house right off campus near the frat houses, and the game plan was for me, Chris, Justin, and Gord to stay there. My dad knew about the wild adventures that Chris and I had gotten into and so he thought it would be a good idea for Gord to stay with us and keep us out of trouble. My dad thought since Gord was now a professional baseball player, he had matured from his wild college days. Well, although my dad was right most of the time, this time he was wrong because Gord was the craziest partier of us all. Putting the four of us in that house without Dan to keep us in check created a completely out-of-control scene.

It was chaos at that house with Gord there, but Chris, Justin, and I had to focus on football that fall of 2007, with the season coming up. I didn't party and focused instead on my training. Football practice was starting, my freshman year was here, and I didn't want to sit on the bench. I had come to Arizona because I wanted to start that opening game. I was determined as a freshman to let everyone know right away that I was going to be the best college tight end ever.

4

FRESHMAN FOOTBALL

I didn't go to college just to party with hot chicks. As I said, I went to Arizona so that I could play football right away as a freshman and go to the NFL. As much fun as it was to be around my brothers and be the big shot on campus, I was focused on football. I didn't want to be the big-time high school recruit who was all hype and becomes a bust. I had my share of fun with the guys but not until after I worked hard with my weight training, with my running, and with my playbook.

But make no mistake, football was my priority. Playing football meant studying film, constantly reading my playbook, and keeping my grades up. It also meant weight lifting, running, practicing, etc. . . . I took care of business first. And business was all about being dominant. Everything about me stands for being fearless and the best. Whether I am the best football player or the best at whatever me and my boys are doing at the moment, the Gronkowskis always want to compete and win.

That first college football practice was the ultimate competition for me. I had never before faced a challenge like I did that first football practice. To understand why, you have to know right off the bat that the very first college football practice is something special. Everyone on the team wants to see if the freshmen can play or if they suck. You can tell right away who's tough and who's a wimp, who's athletic and who's sorry, who's strong and who's weak, who's hard-nosed and who's soft, who's going to make it and who isn't. All the upperclassmen talk trash, challenge the freshmen, and try to intimidate them. And that's how it should be. The young guys need to be toughened up and hardened by fire. This is football, where it's all about mental toughness and imposing your will against your opponent. That feeling of grabbing someone, wrestling them, beating them, and throwing them down is one of the best. I love it!

That first freshman practice is crazy because you aren't going up against high school kids from the neighborhood anymore. You are now going up against Division 1 players from all over the country. It kind of feels like your whole football future is decided with that first practice. Football meant everything to me. It was my whole way of life. I studied, stayed out of trouble, lifted weights, trained with positional drills, ran mile after mile, and pushed myself to the limit all these years so that I could keep playing football. And I didn't just want to be on the team. I wanted to make plays. I wanted to dominate. I wanted to block guys onto their back. I wanted to score touchdowns. I wanted to follow in my dad's and brothers' footsteps and take it to a whole new level. I wanted everyone to be proud of me. But most of all, I love the game and wanted to play it better than anyone had before.

So I felt huge pressure on me going into that first practice. I was supposed to be a hotshot freshman with the highest expectations. I was now 6′6″ and bigger than ever at 270 pounds of all muscle. That is monstrously huge for a freshman tight end, or a senior or even an NFL tight end. Thanks to my training and super-hyped dancing, although I was huge at 270 pounds, I had no excess weight and my six-pack was tight.

Physically, I was feeling faster, stronger, and more explosive than ever. All my physical attributes, all my experiences of being tested at Pittsburgh and matching up against my brothers, had me mentally ready. But until you put your hand in the dirt, line up across from your opponent, and go at it, you are going to be nervous that first freshman practice and I was no exception. I wasn't scared that I wasn't good enough or that I didn't have what it took. I was scared not to be who I was supposed to be. I was scared not to meet my expectations of being good enough to play as a freshman.

What made that first practice even more intimidating is that I was supposed to match up against the defense's best athlete, senior defensive end Louis Holmes, who was one of the best prospects in the country. As I said, I knew this wasn't high school anymore, where I had the huge physical advantage of being a man among boys. This was Division 1 and Louis was one of the top pass rushers in the nation. The guy was tall, strong, and fast, built like a freak. The question everyone wanted to know the answer to was whether I was strong enough, quick enough, talented enough, and tough enough to block him. A lot of players and coaches thought Louis would get the best of me.

The two of us were lined up against each other right away that first practice. When the moment came, when the challenge was there, it was just like matching up against my brothers. I didn't think too much, I just focused on getting my hands on him and using my strength and size to block him. I knew how to block and stayed with what I had been taught. I didn't get too emotional. When the ball was snapped, he exploded into me faster and stronger than I had ever experienced before, but I could handle it. I stayed in front of him and got in his way. At first, I couldn't believe how fast his get-off was for his size and strength. We kept going and going and each time I got better. I learned how to use my body to wall him off. I wasn't blocking him with my hands yet; I wasn't good enough. But I worked and worked and worked until I could block with good technique and use my strength instead of just my size.

From those practices, I gained immense confidence that I could block anyone in college football. Louis was good, and he challenged me and had some good rushes, but I got better each time in practice. Going up against him was great training for me as a blocker. It prepared me for blocking the upcoming defensive ends.

After getting the job done as a blocker, when it came time to run routes in practice, I was super-confident. This was going to be easy, I thought. That first snap, I was a lot taller than the linebacker across from me. I was fired up and couldn't wait to run right by the guy. So I was completely shocked when the ball was hiked and he jammed me at the line and I couldn't get past him. He got his hands into my shoulder pads, got low, and pressed against my shoulder pads upward so I was upright and couldn't use my legs. I had never been jammed before like that and was embarrassed. I knew I was bigger, stronger, quicker, and faster than he was but he had technique and I didn't. I was pissed off and wanted to fight but I knew the way to win was to learn the technique. So I worked with my position coach, Dana Dimel, all week on using my hands to keep my opponents' hands off me.

It was like learning hand slapping. The idea is to utilize the swim move as the way to get off the jam. The technique is to take a step in one direction with your right foot as if you are going to the right, use your left hand to push his hands and body to that right direction, and use the force of his resistance to break left with your other foot as you push off with your left hand and then use your right hand to come up over and down like a swimming technique as you drive your right shoulder away from him. The key is that it is not just using your hands, but using your feet, arms, shoulders, head fake, and legs all in synch together, with perfect timing. The technique has to be perfectly coordinated from your head to your toes or you will be stonewalled at the line.

Beating the jam is just like wrestling; it's more about technique than it is raw strength. The moves have to be fast, precise, accurate, and perfectly timed, and that requires repetition through intense training. It really comes down to training. I had been trained to block. I had been trained to catch. I had not been trained coming out of high school to beat the jam. So I worked with the veteran tight ends, went against the dummy, a teammate holding a big pad, just worked with everyone I could on it to make it like second nature where I was superfast at it. Practicing all day every day for about a week got me to the point where I was solid at getting off the jam. But to get good, I needed game-time training.

The key thing about me and my game is my training. I have been trained over and over again since I was a little kid to be strong, tough, athletic, and fearless. I was trained to play sports. But I also had one other key edge. My dad wanted us to get the best training we could as teenagers, so he took us to Demeris Johnson.

Demeris had been a professional athlete, playing wide receiver in the NFL for the Miami Dolphins in the early 1990s. My dad told Demeris to be supertough on us and he was. Our conditioning and our mind-set for training were as good as anyone's in the country for our age. Demeris put us through grueling workouts to push us to do more than what we thought we could do. He pushed us and pushed us until we learned to love pushing ourselves. As we got older, we got stronger and kept reaching new heights. Instead of getting the regular training of playing sports, we got specialized professional training and that gave us a huge edge. The mental toughness and discipline we learned was critical because it taught me if I couldn't do something today, if I set my mind to it, I could do it tomorrow. And it was that mind-set that kept me working to beat the jam and push linebackers around who would try to jam me.

My teammates thought I was better than they were because I was more athletically gifted with size, speed, and coordination. Maybe, maybe not. I know that I was better because I was better trained. I outperformed everyone because I outworked everyone. I learned that from Demeris, my dad, and my brothers. When I was younger and lost to my older brothers, I learned to keep working, to get better, and started to win. Hard work is why I was better. There are other people in this world with better physical genetics than I have, but they weren't lucky enough to have a dad and brothers like I did to help me make the most of my gifts. They didn't have the training I had. Like I said, it's all about the training. No one trains harder than I do.

When I learned to get off the jam and run my routes, I had another problem—I wasn't getting open. The defense focused on covering me and the linebacker and the safety double-covered me. Getting open isn't just about running fast; it's about faking out your opponent. The key is to know when to change directions and which direction to go in. Running a route isn't just going ten yards and turning around. If you are where your defender thinks you will be, he will either intercept the ball or hit you so hard you won't be able to hang on to it.

As a tight end, you have defenders running full speed at you from different directions. If you are in their path when the ball comes, they will de-cleat you and knock you on your butt.

The key is gaining separation. You gain separation by accelerating away from your opponent. If the opponent thinks you are going to run straight down the field, he will run down the field with you and he will have a head start with a good angle and be able to use his body to shield you from the ball. However, if you make him think you are going to run straight downfield and he runs full speed with you, and then when he is fully committed with all his momentum, you plant your foot hard in the ground and break away to the other side, you will have separation for a moment until he can catch up to you.

The tough part about being a receiver is that you are depending on your quarterback to throw it to where you will have separation. Your quarterback has to anticipate where the defender will be and throw it where he won't be. So while I may break away from the linebacker, I may be running right into the path of a safety coming down hill full speed to take my head off. The key is for the quarterback to get the ball to me after I separate from the linebacker and before the safety can hit me. If the throw is timed right, I can catch it and protect myself from the hitter and make the play.

Remember, my senior year of high school in Pittsburgh, all I did was block. As a freshman at Arizona, I had to learn how to get off the jam and then run the route to gain separation. I practiced and practiced running routes. I watched film to understand what are the best routes against certain types of coverage. A basic route is the seam route, where the tight end looks for the opening in the defense and runs toward that spot. The quarterback and tight end are both supposed to read and see the defense to know where

IT'S GOOD TO BE GRONK

that spot will be. The spot is typically between the two hashmarks in the middle of the field and is typically past the linebackers and in between the two split safeties. It's like finding the center of a triangle. There is always an opening in the defense, but it won't be there for long because as soon as the safety sees you, he moves in to close the gap. It is up to me to get to that seam and it is up to the quarterback to get the ball to me the moment the seam is open and before it closes. Remember that the safety and linebacker are coming full speed at me and looking to break me in half. I am a sitting duck until the ball gets there, and as long as I have a step or two to see the hit coming and brace for it, I can handle it.

My first game as a freshman was a big thrill, the chance to wear that Arizona uniform and helmet. My coach started me as a true freshman in my first game and that was very rare, since only a few true freshmen start that first game. The biggest reason why it's so rare is that the coaches have to be able to trust the true freshman to know the playbook and the system, read the defenses, to be on the same page with his teammates and not make big mistakes. If I run to the right when I am supposed to run to the left, the quarterback will throw an interception and that could cost us the game. If I run a route instead of staying in to block because I got the play wrong, I could get our quarterback hurt. If I block the defender to the right when I am supposed to block him to the left, I could get our running back hurt. These are players' health and college careers on the line. One bad injury is all it takes, and too often injuries happen because of mistakes where someone doesn't block the man they were supposed to. Coaches also need to win to keep their jobs and nothing makes a coach look worse than mental mistakes by their players, so coaches are very reluctant to play freshmen until the coaches are comfortable and confident enough that the player knows what he is doing.

That first game to start the 2007 season was against Brigham Young University, on the road. As luck would have it, Gord had been playing professional baseball for the Orem Owls in Orem, Utah. The Owls are the minor-league team in the Pioneer League for the Los Angeles Angels. My game was in Provo and started at 4 p.m. Gord's game was at 7 p.m. at the Owls' stadium, which was just up the road from BYU. It was freak luck for me and Gord that my opening game was right near his park. Gord got the okay from his coach to go to the start of my game, stayed for the first three quarters, and then went and played in his game.

With Gord and my parents there for my first game, I was fired up but nervous. I didn't want to make any mistakes. I wanted to do well in front of my family and show my coaches they were right to trust me. We ran the ball early on and that helped me get a little more comfortable on each down. It seemed like all I did the first two quarters was block. The BYU guys I went up against weren't better than Louis Holmes, so I was ready for them. It was fun to push, fight, wrestle, and mix it up. I was stronger, faster, and better trained than my opponent but I had to battle like hell to win. Ninety percent wasn't good enough. I had to go 100 percent on every single play because I learned from matching up against Louis that if I went 90 percent on one play, that one play is going to be a sack or a tackle for a loss. I wasn't going to be embarrassed and let that happen. I liked my quarterback and teammates. I wanted to earn their respect and I was going to fight harder than anyone to get it.

It was on the very first play after kickoff in the third quarter that the coach finally called my number. It was first down and our kickoff return man had returned the ball to get it to our 29-yard line. When our quarterback, Willie Tuitama, called the play, I knew there was a good chance it would go to me. I felt huge pressure to get open and catch the ball. I was thinking, Oh man, I need to get this, I gotta catch this and show everyone what I am about.

So when the ball was snapped, I ran straight up the field and my eyes got huge when I saw the ball come my way. I focused intensely on that ball from the second it left Willie's hand until it went into my hands. I could see the laces and pigskin spiral like it was in slow motion. I looked the ball all the way in until I had it wrapped in my arms. I got hit right after catching it and ran through the first hit and the second guy tackled me. I had done it so many times that it should have been easy, but I felt so much pressure that it was challenging. That's not the mind-set you want. You don't want to be thinking, Oh boy, I better catch this, but that's how it was for me. I was so happy when I got up because when I caught the ball and broke the first tackle, I broke through that tight mental barrier. When I got up, I went back to the huddle much more confident and relaxed. I was still hyped but not scared. That catch, making that play, helped me get free-minded, which is how I need to play the game. I was able to get those first-catch jitters out of the way, a crucial step forward.

Unfortunately we lost that game, 20–7, but our first home game was next and I was fired up for next Saturday. We didn't have a tunnel at Arizona Stadium, but we ran through two lines of cheerleaders and it was the most exciting thing in the world to me. I was beyond hyped up, and just wanted to smash somebody, anybody on the other side of the field. We were playing Northern Arizona and were strong favorites. I was much more confident, much more comfortable; being on our home field was an entirely different feeling from that first game. I had two big catches that game. One was for 39 yards and another was a 26-yard touchdown in the third quarter. I was amazed at what a difference a week could make. The previous week, I was nervous and scared to fail. This week I was confident and when the ball was in the air, it just came natural and easy to me. On the touchdown, I didn't know I was going to score until I caught it and turned around toward the end zone and saw a clear path in front of me. I had been wide open and couldn't wait for the ball to come my way. As soon as I caught it, I ran straight into the end zone untouched. That first touchdown felt great. I knew that I deserved to be out there, that I was on the field because I was good, not because I was a hotshot recruit. It was a huge confidence builder and we won the game 45–24.

Coming off my first touchdown I was overconfident; I thought I knew what I was doing, but I was wrong. We lost the next game at home to New Mexico, which was really disappointing. I had only two catches, for 13 yards, and no touchdowns. I thought things would automatically get better with each game but that wasn't the case. I had a hard time getting open because I didn't know the ropes yet. I didn't really know how to run routes and get open. I made a few freshman mistakes and it was a tough game.

The next week was even worse. We lost on the road to California and I had no catches. Again I had a hard time getting open and the ball didn't come my way. But I didn't get down on myself or lose confidence. I kept working with my tight end coach Dana Dimel and busting my butt in practice to improve my route running and understand how to get open.

The thing about me is I stay positive. I love to work hard and play the game, so I believe in grinding hard to turn things around. That's exactly what happened the next game on the road, where we beat Washington State. It was a huge game for me. After having no catches the week before, I put up four catches for 115 yards and two touchdowns. The first touchdown was for 18 yards in the second quarter and gave us a ten-point lead. It was a perfect throw over the middle. I went up, caught it high, took the hit at the goal line, and scored. It seemed easy to me.

On the next drive, I caught a short pass over the middle, bobbled it, and then got hold of it. As soon as I had control over the ball, I got hit on my left and bounced off, then on my right, bounced off that, then ran through a third tackle until the fourth guy grabbed my legs. My confidence was soaring and I was having fun. To me it was no harder than anything else I had done before, but now it was Division 1 college on TV, in front of thousands of people cheering for me.

It was a far cry from being that freshman who was scared to make a mistake. Now I couldn't wait for the ball to come to me so

I could make the play and score. I was fired up and wanted more. My quarterback, Willie, threw it to me again in the fourth quarter. I ran deep over the middle of the field. The ball was snapped at our 43-yard line and I ran straight down the field. It was a deep ball on a seam route between the safeties and I caught it around the twenty-yard line. I knew the safety was coming down hard to hit me on my side but he bounced off me, knocking himself out. I stumbled and was off balance but I regained my footing and sprinted another twenty yards into the end zone before the other defenders could catch me.

That was a breakout game for me. That was the type of performance I knew I was capable of delivering. I got my chance to show what kind of player I am and made the most of it. I broke tackles, made the tough catch over the middle in traffic, and scored. That game showed me I could be dominant at the college level.

And then, wouldn't you know it, we lost the next game and I had no catches. I was on a huge roller-coaster ride of up-and-down games. I was blocking well and catching the ball well, but I was still making my share of mistakes and was nowhere close to reaching my potential. I wasn't running the wrong routes but I wasn't running them as smart as I could, as precisely as I could, and getting the separation I should have gotten. I had a lot to learn and it was a tough adjustment being ready to roll on every play of every game. I was blocking and battling in the trenches and every time it was exhausting because I gave it my all on every play.

It was very different from high school. Dealing with traveling across the country, the away-game atmosphere, precise routines, and tight schedules—it was demanding and took a lot out of me. I was still learning how to read defenses and find the open spot and sometimes the defenses weren't easy to read, either.

The next game was a tough loss at number-ten-ranked USC, where I had one catch for seven yards and fumbled it. I caught the ball and the safety came at me hard. I wanted to give him a shot back and I did, but I wasn't protecting the ball. These linebackers, defensive linemen, and safeties were fast, too. Everyone can hit and everyone can tackle. That fumble made me very aware that first and foremost I have to protect the ball, so I worked on that in practice as a fundamental part of my game.

We lost again at home to Stanford, our third loss in a row. I had another down game with two catches and no touchdowns. After three straight losses and unimpressive outings by me, I decided, that Thursday night before the upcoming game versus Washington, to finally party with my brothers. I really hadn't partied during the season and I was feeling like I needed to break with the routine in order to get out of this funk, so I had some fun with my boys. I got crazy, way overdid it, and drank way too much. I woke up the next morning and had the worst hangover ever. Fortunately, Friday's practice was always light and easy so I was able to get through it okay. The big problem was that come game day, Saturday, I still felt super-hungover. I had never had a hangover that lasted two days and was shocked. I felt sick and didn't want to play but I couldn't let my team down just because I drank too much that Thursday night before, so I toughed it out.

To compensate for the hangover, I really focused on my technique in blocking and in running routes. I couldn't rely on raw strength and speed. I had to use technique and somehow I played really well. I caught a 51-yard touchdown pass to tie up the score in the second quarter. I caught it over the middle and I was like, Thank you, Lord, for letting me get so wide open that no one touched me. I did not want to get hit and was thankful to score without getting hit. My blocking was good enough, not great, but we won the game. I had three catches for 85 yards, including the big 51-yard touchdown, so I still did my part to help my team win, but I didn't drink again for the rest of the season. I was not going to make that mistake again.

Yup, that freshman year was a learning experience, but it was time to get off the roller coaster and stay on top. I made sure to have a good week of practice and we had a huge win at home versus UCLA. For the first time all season, we had two wins in a row and I had two big games in a row. That game I had six catches for 94 yards, with a 27-yard touchdown, but what was the most fun was how I ran through and broke tackles. I wanted to show the country that no one could tackle me. I was jumping over defenders, jumping high to catch the ball; I ran through five tacklers on one play to get the first down and keep the chains moving. I had a big fourth-quarter catch for 27 yards where I made a high leaping catch that helped run down the clock for the win. It was a close game, 34–27, and a hard-fought victory. That was a complete game for me in all phases: blocking, catching, breaking tackles, scoring, and dominating the defense.

And we did it again the next week at home with a huge win over second-ranked Oregon.

I had good stats, with five catches for 73 yards, but the key play for me was late in the fourth quarter on a third down with four yards to go. There was around seven minutes left to play and we were up 31–24. We were at our 39-yard line and did not want to punt and give them good field position with enough time to score and tie it up. I didn't know if the ball was coming to me and the play was designed for me to run a short route where as soon as the ball is snapped I run across the field about five yards deep, just past the first-down marker. I looked at the coverage as I lined up waiting on the snap and I wasn't optimistic that there would be an opening. The linebacker was waiting on me to run toward him and was anticipating the cross route, so after taking a couple of steps after the snap, I broke off the route, planted my foot to stop, and turned 180 degrees to run back the other way. The danger of changing the route is that if Willie throws it before I make my change of direction then it will be picked off, because I won't be there. But I knew that Willie wouldn't throw it, because I was running right into coverage and was not open. So Willie saw me read the defense and go the other way. We were really on the same page. I exploded out of my cut, accelerating away from the linebacker, and got separation. Willie fired it right in there and I caught it and ran down the field for a sixteen-yard gain.

We ended up driving down for a field goal and won the game. That play showed I wasn't a freshman anymore and was a football-smart player. Willie had trust in me and it was a huge play to seal the win.

We had now won three games in a row and had a chance to finish 6-6 if we won our final game against our biggest rival, Arizona State. We wanted to win this game bad. We weren't going to a bowl game, since our record wasn't good enough, so this last game would be our finale.

We started the game off strong, with me scoring a touchdown in the first quarter on a one-yard pass from Willie. Unfortunately, after that first quarter, we never had the lead again and lost, 20–17. I finished the game with two catches for 29 yards with the touchdown, but that was a very painful loss and a bad way to end the season. ASU did a good job of scheming for me, and our offense just couldn't get anything going until it was too late. I finished the season with 28 catches for 525 yards and six touchdowns, which was up and down, but the bottom line was our team went 5-7, and that sucked.

It was a long season with road games and tough losses. I knew I needed to be more consistent. I couldn't have games with zero or only one or two catches. I had to be a force in every game. I also had to do something else—party! The season was over and it was time to have fun with my brothers.

5

CLUB G

Okay, here's the deal: football season was over, it had its ups and downs, but I had busted my butt and now it was time to move forward. That meant it was time to train for next season and party for tonight. The good thing about the way me and my brothers party is that we don't sit on our butts or just stand around with drinks in our hands. We go hard! We don't do drugs; we don't need to. We have so much energy and are so fired up just to party among ourselves that whether there is alcohol or not, we jump at the chance to get wild and start dancing to the extreme, laughing, making jokes, doing stupid things, and having so much fun it is infectious to everyone around us. Because when we get started, we party harder than anybody. We are dancing high-energy, constant moves, jumping, gyrations—it is the best cardio workout ever. So actually, even when I am partying, I am working out.

I don't care who you are, where you go, and what you do: no one can party like Gord. This guy loves to go out, hang out, drink a few drinks, dance crazy with the ladies, and have fun like no one else. Now, at the time I'm talking about, since Gord was playing professional baseball in the minors, he had money, while the rest of us were on a strict budget. Gord always had that extra hundred bucks to buy kegs and do fun things. With Gord there, every night that spring and summer was a party, and I mean *every* night.

At our house, the front door and back door were perfectly aligned to form a straight line right through the living room, kitchen, and hallway. The hallway was a tiled floor. So what Gord would do to get the party started was create a hundred-foot-long slip-and-slide. We would invite all the hot athletic and sorority girls over, then take dishwashing liquid and squirt it all over the floor to make it slippery. We would then squirt it all over ourselves to get lubed up and then throw water all over the place. The name of the game was to make it from door to door sliding on your chest, and the only way to make it was to get a fast head start. The hallway was wide enough to make it through without crashing into the wall, and since we were all in great shape, it didn't really hurt. Having alcohol in our systems made it even more fun. And the girls loved coming over to do it. The rules were the guys had to strip down to their underwear and the girls had to strip down to their panties and bras. They knew that if they were coming over to our place, they were going to slip and slide. The ladies loved doing the slide but couldn't go headfirst. They had to slide feetfirst on their back-sides because otherwise their chests caused too much resistance and slowed them down. Whichever way you did it, something was always coming off. Somebody was always naked and the girls loved it when our underwear slid off. We had those slip-and-slides all the time at Club G. That's what we called our house.

To make Club G even more fun, we were always incorporating drinking games with the slip-and-slide. We formed tag teams where a girl and guy would be on each team and the object of the game was to slide from the back door to the table, chug a quart of beer, flip the cup (like the game flip cup), and then slide back and tag your partner; then your partner would do the same. Whichever team made it back to the door first, won. We called it flip-and-slip.

This one time, and for some reason no one can remember, Gord switched his underwear with a girl and wore her thong to do the competition. Gord went first and finished, racing through the front door to win. He was superexcited about winning, until he stood up and saw a police officer standing right there. Gord just stood there in the girl's thong and said, "Oh, uh . . . hi, Officer. Is there a problem?"

I don't know how the officer kept a straight face, but he did and said there had been a noise complaint. Gord asked if he could go in the front door to put his pants on, but since he had had one too many drinks, he grabbed the girl's jeans instead of his. He got the pants halfway up his legs until he realized they were hers and not his, and then fell over laughing. Years later, in my second year as a New England Patriot, I did a Christmas show on TV called

Shopping with Gronk. I went shopping for the family, and for Gord I bought a thong at Victoria's Secret. Now you know why.

There was always a party going on at our place. Our deal was we had to have what we called a pregame party, where we had a few girls come over and start the drinking, dancing, and just getting wild. Then we would go to wherever the happening party was, and when that was over we would come back to our place for the after party. I was always hungry by the time we came back for the after party, so for whatever reason, one I really can't explain, every party night you could find me cooking scrambled eggs totally naked at 2 or 3 a.m. I made them for the whole crew as the designated egg maker.

Well, it wasn't literally every night, since my parents would visit from time to time and when that happened, we toned things down somewhat.

When my dad, aka Big G or Papa Gronk, first visited us, he walked in the door and saw a girl sliding completely naked down the hallway. Big G looked at Gord and knew he had miscalculated in sending Gord there to keep us out of trouble. As hard as we tried, we never got my dad to do the slip-and-slide, but he had fun watching everyone else do it.

When my mom visited she wasn't a happy camper at all. Club G was furnished with a hot tub in the front yard, under a tree. The price of admission for the ladies to get into Club G's hot tub was to throw their bra or bikini top into the tree. When my mom visited, she saw all the bras in the tree and was pissed. When we were kids, she used to threaten us or hit us with a hard, big plastic spoon to do her best to stop us from doing whatever we were doing. I could swear she instinctively reached for that spoon when she saw the tree. If she had had it, she would have come after us.

It was great having the hot sorority girls party with us at Club G, but it pissed off the frat guys who were supposed to be getting with them. Fraternities and football players don't get along; that's just the way it is on college campuses. I had made a mistake as a freshman in going by myself to one particular frat party. Some frat guy's girl was getting overly friendly with me and the guy didn't like it. I didn't know it at the time, but these guys had it out for me. After having a few drinks, I went to the bathroom to take a leak. When I came out, no less than eight guys jumped me and hit me with whatever they could get their hands on.

Chris and Justin weren't there, I was by myself in enemy territory and that was a big problem. My first thought, other than wondering what hit me, was that I didn't want to get into trouble with my coach and get suspended. My second thought was to get the hell out of there. I instinctively punched, kicked, and threw four of the guys out of my way, but a bunch more guys jumped on me. Guys were coming at me from behind and from all angles; it was a battle to get out of there. Eventually eight of them got me to the ground and I was taking kicks everywhere, but our quarterback, Willie Tuitama, was there, and when he saw what was going on, he helped get me out of there. The girl I had been friendly with told me that I looked like the Hulk throwing four dudes off me.

She loved it and definitely made it up to me later. So other than a slight black eye, I didn't really get hurt, but still I never made that mistake again of being solo in enemy territory.

When I told Chris, Gord, and Justin what happened, they went nuts. The whole team found out right away and went down there to beat the hell out of each and every one of those frat guys. When we got there, Chris and Gord were screaming at them to come and fight. They wouldn't come out; they were scared to death. We made sure not to step on their property so they couldn't get us in trouble with the cops, but they called the cops on us anyway and we had to get out of there.

That wasn't the end of it with the frat houses. Another frat had a big party a few weeks later and we knew better than to go into their house. There were fifty guys there. So, not looking for trouble, we stayed in the street and didn't go on their property. It was a big party so there were girls in the front yard, inside the house, in the backyard; they were everywhere and there were plenty for everyone.

My roommate Justin Salum and one of our teammates were out front with me as well. Ten frat guys started talking trash to our teammate. He wasn't looking for trouble and laughed it off, keeping things cool, but the biggest frat guy there, some 6'5" dude, threw a full beer can and hit our teammate in the head. Grabbing his head, he stayed on his feet but staggered back and was momentarily dazed. Justin saw who did it and charged the frat guy, grabbing him by the throat. The frat guy punched Justin in his left eye and then all hell broke loose. Justin threw a right hook and decked the guy.

The crowd started yelling, "Fight! Fight!" and no less than twenty frat guys came running out of the house. It was thirty of those frat guys versus ten of us, but we hated them and didn't hold back. This was an all-out rumble in the middle of the street. I had seen the movie *The Outsiders* with Matt Dillon, which had an awesome rumble scene, but this was even better. There was blood flying, bodies getting slammed, alcohol spilling, and women screaming everywhere.

All I know is Chris and I saw Justin deck that guy and we knew there was only one way out of there and that was to fight our way out. We were surrounded and getting jumped. With Chris right next to me, we were punching, kicking, tackling, throwing, and just messing dudes up! It was the wildest fight ever. Chris and I got into Hulk mode and smashed guys! Our other roommate, Orlando Vargas, was a big football player, too, and he was a force to be reckoned with out there. Orlando was a monster! While I was body-slamming a guy into the side of a car, another frat guy knocked me into the car, and I banged my elbow pretty hard, but other than that, the worst injury we had was Justin's black eye. The other frat houses hated that frat, so those frat boys were cheering us on as we were beating the other ones' butts. The cops got there but we got home, our shirts bloodied, and didn't get into trouble. That was the last fight I've gotten into, but it ranks as the all-time best.

6

ALL BUSINESS

Sure, I had my share of fun in the off-season at Club G, but once the fall of 2008 came rolling around, that meant training camp for sophomore year of football was here and I was a man on a mission. I was proud of what I had accomplished as a freshman, where my 18.8 yards average per reception led the team and I set a school tight end record with 525 total yards receiving. Being named to the *Sporting News* freshman all-American team, the Rivals.com freshman all-American team, the *Sporting News* freshman Pac-10 team, and the All-Pac-10 honorable mention team was nice bragging rights, but I wasn't happy with my year. I wanted to show my parents, my brothers, and my friends that I was the best. It wasn't about me trying to prove my doubters wrong. It was all about me proving my people right. My people also included my training coach Demeris Johnson.

When I was in the eighth grade, my dad wanted us to get more serious about our potential. My dad's goal was for all of us to get scholarships, but for me he had special plans. My dad had heard that Demeris Johnson was a good trainer, and he had just finished playing in the NFL. Demeris played wide receiver for three years with the Dolphins from 1993 through 1996, and then spent a year with the Buffalo Bills. Demeris was new in town and had been a professional trainer for about a year when my dad went to one of his training sessions at a nearby high school that let him use their facilities. My dad was very impressed with the session and knew right away that Demeris was the real deal as a trainer.

At the time, Gord was away at school in Florida at Jacksonville University on a baseball scholarship. Dan was a senior in high school, Chris was a junior, and I was in eighth grade. My dad told Demeris that he wanted him to train Dan and Chris so they would get football scholarships. He then introduced me to Demeris and asked him if he could make me the number-one tight end recruit in the country. Demeris looked at me and said to my dad with dead-serious intensity, "I can do that."

Demeris then turned to me and asked me, "Are you willing to commit right here and now to work superhard for the next four years to become that number-one recruit?" I was ready to work and had wanted to be the best even before I walked in the door. My dad had instilled in the four of us to compete with one another, to go all-out to win, to work hard, to be the best and never give up.

But just as important, we pushed each other, we rooted for each other; there was never any jealousy or animosity. We were family and knew what that meant, but we still wanted to beat the hell out of each other every chance we could get.

We had that mind-set before we met Demeris, but Demeris helped take it to the next level. He and my dad sat down that day and put together a four-year plan with speed and agility training to make me that number-one recruit. We followed that plan from start to finish. About eight weeks into eighth grade, my oldest brother, Gord, came up from Jacksonville to visit with us. When we told Gord how tough our workout regimen was he laughed it off, saying he could handle it, no problem.

Gord wasn't laughing after long. In fact, he started puking after we had run six of the 400-yard sprints. The workout was a Monday workout, which was always the toughest. When we first started, Demeris would have us run four 400-yard sprints where we had to make it in 1:15 for each sprint. So we had eight weeks of training where we gradually increased our 400-yard sprints from a set of four to a set of eight. Gord handled the first four, but couldn't make the time on the fifth and on the sixth; he was hanging over the side of a waist-high fence puking his guts out. He then collapsed onto his back. We started razzing Gord and got him good. We dunked a Gatorade bucket of ice water on him and laughed at him uncontrollably. He told us he would get up and finish, while we hysterically teased him. To Gord's credit, he did get up and ran the full set of eight and somehow finished. From that point on we all had the utmost respect for Demeris's workouts because they did nothing but get tougher and tougher on us. And by the way, I became that number-one high school tight end recruit thanks in no small part to our training from Demeris.

But it was those expectations from early on and that kind of support I had from my family and friends that made me set the highest expectations for myself. I was cocky about my abilities but not arrogant toward others; there's a difference. I wanted to be the best tight end in college football and believed that I could be that guy. It wasn't about me being better than anyone else; it was about me being my best. And even though I did some good things my freshman year, it was too much of a roller-coaster ride of ups and downs. I had some games where was I absolutely dominant and then others where I wasn't a factor at all. The inconsistency was what bothered me. The way I saw it, inconsistent results come from inconsistent training, so I knew from growing up in my house that there's only one way to get better—work harder.

I worked at becoming a better blocker and route runner. I knew if I wanted the ball more in games, I would have to convince my coaches by having great practices. So now I was nineteen and had a full year of Arizona under my belt. I was much more confident because I understood so much more about playing college football. I realized that the intensity I had in practice, in the weight room, and everywhere else would carry over to the game.

Chris and I were in the training room every day that summer. We worked as hard or harder than anyone else on the team, lifting weights and then running. I wanted to get my body ready for the grind of a long season and knew what it would take. Having Chris as my workout partner was awesome. Every day was a fun competition in the gym with Chris, where we were talking smack and getting amped over who was stronger, who could lift more, who had bigger muscles or the better six-pack. Chris made everything fun and we were always joking around and having a good time while busting our butts. We had challenges over who could bench-press more, curl more, squat more, dead-lift more, and everything else you could lift in the gym. It was extremely productive; we were gym rats.

When I wasn't in the gym with Chris, I was working on running routes. Sometimes I would run routes against my teammates and other times I would run them on air (by myself with the quarterback throwing me the ball). Having that full spring practice under my belt was huge for me. I learned to appreciate the value of running seven-on-sevens, which is offense versus defense but without the offensive or defensive lines. In seven-on-sevens, you really get to work on your route running and it challenges you to run them precisely, since otherwise you won't get open.

Having a whole off-season to practice working on my routes, to watch game film, to get faster and stronger, made a huge difference in my confidence. A confident player is a dominant player. A scared player is a defeated player. The more prepared you are, the more confident you are. The more confident you are, the more fearless you are. The more fearless you are, the more focused and precise your actions will be. The more precise your entire body movement is, the greater your speed and separation will be. Precision is everything because wasted motions only slow you down.

Learning all these technical details is what makes the difference between being trained versus untrained. And the trained talented athlete will always beat the untrained talented athlete. Doing all this over and over again made a world of difference for my confidence and I could not have been more ready for the start of training camp my sophomore year.

I got up at 5:15 a.m. every day to eat breakfast and be on the field ready for the 6:15 a.m. practice and then on to 9 a.m. classes. Since practice was so early, it wasn't overly hot, which we all appreciated. There was no partying, no drinking, no nothing but football. I was off to my best start, and then out of the blue I got hit with mono, which was devastating for me. Only two weeks away from the start of the season and I was out of commission. I couldn't understand how I got it, because I did everything I was supposed to do. I wasn't partying; I was working out, getting my sleep, eating right, doing all the right things. It was just a bad break and I had no choice but to roll with the punches. Those first three weeks of being sick, my throat was killing me, I had no energy, I was weak, I lost weight, and I was sleepy all the time. I was sleeping eighteen hours a day, in fact. That might sound appealing but it wasn't.

I watched that first game up in the press box with the coaches. It was a home game and we beat Idaho 70–0. The reality of watching my teammates play and seeing the football world move on without me was agonizing. After all the hard work I had put in during the off-season, to get in the best shape of my life and then miss that first game was a miserable experience. I wanted to be out there with my teammates and be part of the win and the celebrating, not up in the press box, far from the action.

However, it was a different perspective seeing the game from up high instead of down on the field. I could see the play develop, see the designed openings and the overall big picture of why offensive plays were called and worked. It gave me an improved understanding of what coaches look for and see. Still, it hurt bad to miss it.

At least I could start practicing after the first game and the aches, pains, weakness, fatigue, and all that started going away. I gained back whatever weight I had lost and my body recovered quickly.

Although I worked hard and got a lot better that week of practice, the doctor wouldn't clear me because my spleen was still expanded from the mono. The doctor told me if I took a hit while my spleen was still expanded, it would be vulnerable and could easily pop. If that happened, he told me, it could end my career. So once again, I had to miss the game, but we won at home again versus Toledo, 41–16. I watched this game on the sidelines, which was more fun since I could at least be with my teammates.

That third week, I got my strength and endurance back up to where I wanted it, but the doctor said I needed to take off one more game to let the swelling in my spleen go down. I traveled with the team but felt helpless and pissed off since I could only stand on the sideline and watch my teammates lose at New Mexico 36–28. We should have won that game and I should have been out there to help them do that. Whether it was my fault or not, I felt like I had let the team down because I wasn't out there. I don't like to make excuses, and the bottom line was that I wasn't there to help my teammates. I hated not being there to fight alongside Chris and my teammates but I had to let my spleen settle down.

Finally, I was cleared to play and was like a starving lion let out of a cage after being teased with a steak in front of him for weeks. I couldn't wait to suit up, put the helmet on, run onto the field, hear the roar of the crowd, and get insane.

We were on the road against UCLA. The crowd was loud and although I was far from being one hundred percent, my adrenaline helped make up the difference. I spent the first quarter blocking and getting comfortable, but no passes came my way. At the start of the second quarter, we were down 3–7, but we had the ball and were driving. With the ball at the UCLA 22-yard line, the coach called a play where I run a flag route (same as a corner route). That was my favorite route because I knew the ball was going to come to me if I got open and I knew I could get open all the time on it.

Every time that route is called for me, I'm expecting the ball, and this time was no different. The flag (or corner) route is designed for me to run straight downfield for ten yards, throw a fake head move, and stutter-step inside, but instead break outside heading on a 45-degree angle toward the pylon at the goal line.

When I left the huddle, I was excited but focused. As I lined up, I ran the route in my head, envisioning what I had to do. Willie snapped the ball and I took off. I made my fake move to sell the route and then broke for the pylon at the end zone. I got separation and saw the ball coming my way. I wasn't scared or nervous.

I didn't have the jitters. I was just focused and caught it like I had done a million times before in practice. I made the play, scored the touchdown on my first pass, and we took the lead, 10–7. I felt so relieved and happy to put everything behind me and be back to playing ball.

Later in the fourth quarter, I caught a four-yard touchdown to give us a big lead and we won the game 31–10. I had three catches for 32 yards, which isn't much, but two of those catches were for touchdowns. I couldn't have been happier. I had just a few weeks to get my wind back and my feet under me and it was tough going, but I got through it and we won. I was exhausted when we got home but had to celebrate at Club G with my boys later that night.

To me, life doesn't get any better. I was playing the game I love, my brother was my teammate, we won the game, and now it was time to celebrate. I couldn't have been any happier . . . until the next week.

Playing my first home game of the season had me fired up. The University of Washington Huskies were coming into our backyard and I was ready. Having that extra week of practice really helped me recover and get back to where I was before getting sick. It was a night game and I made it one of the best nights of my life. I matched a school record, catching three touchdowns, and I had five catches for 109 yards and we won 48–14. The first touchdown was a screen pass where my offensive coordinator thought the defense would blitz and they did. It was a great call. I caught a short screen, made a move to break a tackle, and then sprinted in to take it to the house.

Then in the second quarter, we had the ball at Washington's nine-yard line and Willie threw me a short pass over the middle. I hung on to the ball and had to take three hits but fought my way into the end zone. The crowd went wild! From there we just kept rolling and won 48–14.

Next up was Stanford, on the road. We should have won that game, but we didn't. We lost a close one and for whatever reason, I wasn't a factor. I had only two catches for 30 yards and no touchdowns. It was frustrating but all I could do about it was have a good week of practice and get ready for 25th-ranked California back on our home turf.

I had a bad taste in my mouth all week and the only way to get rid of it was to beat a better team (than Stanford) in our backyard. Cal was a tough team; they came to play and were up at halftime 24–14. I had a few catches in the first half but no monster plays. We took the lead in the third quarter, capitalizing on a pick six (interception returned for a touchdown), and were up 35–27 late in the third. On second and seven at the Cal 35-yard line, Coach called the play for me to run a seam route up the middle, full speed. It was a nice throw over the middle and I caught the ball, making the play over the safety. We got the W, beating Cal 42–27. I had 6 catches for 91 yards and it was a sweet win.

What's great about winning is it takes away all the pain from last week's loss. Our record was 5-2 and we were having a strong season with a real chance for a bowl game. We had sixth-ranked USC next and that was a real test for us. They had an NFL-caliber roster on defense and unfortunately we couldn't get anything going on offense. I was frustrated the whole game. They played well together and had a good game plan. I had only two catches for 12 yards and didn't score. Tough loss for us at home, 17–10, to a good team.

The only positive thing about losing a game in the middle of the season is that you get to play again next week to make it right with a win. We had to go on the road to match up against Washington State.

Having only two catches versus USC made me very hungry to get the ball against Washington State. We didn't throw the ball much in the first quarter and did a lot of running, which was working because we were moving the ball. Toward the end of the first quarter, we had the ball at Washington State's 43-yard line. The score was tied and it was a critical third down because we didn't want to punt. We wanted to drive down and score and needed one more first down to get into field goal range. I was frustrated because it was our third drive and I wanted to make plays and help take the game over. With about a minute left in the first quarter, I finally got my shot.

Willie threw me a short pass and I was determined to take it all the way for a 43-yard score. I made guys miss and ran threw the defenders to score the touchdown and take the lead. From there, we never looked back and kept scoring until we won, 59–28. I had a total of four catches for 83 yards, which was solid, but the key is we won and got back on track for getting into a bowl game.

Up next was another game on the road, this time against Oregon, a talented team. We lost that game 55–45 but it was a great game. We were down 45–17 in the first half. The only good part about the first half was that Chris scored on a 37-yard touchdown catch. In the second half, we caught fire and came back to within three points, down 45–48 late in the fourth. That stadium atmosphere was crazy. The students were going wild and the crowd was right on top of you. It was awesome football on both sides of the ball.

Something happened in that second half where I just felt invincible, like I could do anything. I was breaking tackles, running through hits, making crazy catches, throwing guys around with my blocking, and getting open. It's the greatest feeling when you feel so confident, so strong, so fast, so quick, and so explosive that no one can stop you. I felt like I could take on the whole defense. I was in the zone, using spin moves, making people miss, running over people. I was matching up against really good players like Jairus Byrd and Patrick Chung. We had the ball late in the fourth at midfield and we went for it on fourth and three. We didn't convert and never got back in the game. It hurt bad to lose that game. To come back from so far and come so close was brutal, but we played well as a team together that second half. If we had won, that would have been my all-time favorite college game, but we didn't. I wound up with 12 catches for 143 yards and a touchdown, and it was great, until time ran out and we didn't get the W. I won the John Mackey National Tight End of the Week award, but since it was off a loss, I couldn't really enjoy it.

I thought after playing such a good second half against Oregon that we would pick up where we left off and get off to a good start in our next game, but I thought wrong. We were home versus 21st-ranked Oregon State. I had only three catches for 50 yards and a touchdown. We lost 19–17. It was really frustrating to be so inconsistent, where one game our offense was clicking and we were scoring points and then another game we weren't.

The whole season came down to playing our archrival, Arizona State. This year we matched up against them on our home turf. They had beaten us the year before in the final game of the season and we wanted revenge. There was a lot on the line. If we beat them we would get to go to a bowl game for the first time in ten years, which was huge for our school and fans. This time we were fired up and showed up. I scored on a 17-yard touchdown pass and we led 7–0 toward the end of the first. It was a seam route toward the left side of the field. I knew I had to get open and that if the ball came my way I would score. I got open, it came my way, I made a nice catch, hung on to it, and fell down in the end zone. I wound up with six catches for 95 yards and it was a great win. To beat our archrival, to do it at home and with the win get the invitation to play in a bowl game, which hadn't happened for ten years, was the ultimate way to close out the regular season. Now it was on to the Pioneer Las Vegas Bowl.

I know what you are thinking. Me in Vegas for a football game means I was going to have some fun. Well, it didn't happen. We were way too busy and football was the only thing on my mind. I was nineteen and didn't know anything about Vegas but I knew I'd be back, and I was right (I'll get into that later).

For now, we had a monster game to play versus 25th-ranked

BYU and I was all business. We played well as a team and it wasn't one of my best games (4 catches for 27 yards, no TDs) but with a great week of practice we got the win, 31–21, and that was the bottom line. It was a winning year for us to finish 8-5. To close the season with a bowl game win for our fans was a great feeling. Chris had a big game.

Overall, the 2008 season was a step in the right direction. My stats for the year were 47 for 672 and 10 TDs. Five of my touchdowns came in the first two games back after being sick. I had some really good games where I was dominant but I was not dominant in every game, I was not consistent the way I wanted to be. My junior year was coming up and I wanted to break all the records and be the best ever. I had to make it happen.

7

KNOCKED DOWN

Every year in high school and college, I took my game to the next level. I made a huge leap my freshman year, coming out of high school, and an even bigger leap my sophomore year, after I had learned the ropes. Going into my junior year at Arizona in 2009, I was no longer adjusting to the daily challenges of playing college football. In just two seasons, I rewrote the record books at Arizona, setting the school's single-game, season, and career records for receptions, yards, and touchdowns by a tight end. Now I was ready to break NCAA records.

I was completely comfortable and in a great routine with my training. When spring practices came around, I felt strong, elusive, and dominant. I was in the zone and my confidence was at an all-time high. I felt indestructible and knew I would be the best tight end in the country, which was what I had been trained for ever since I was a kid. My coaches knew it, too, and they were going to feature me.

I was also excited because Dan had just been drafted by the Detroit Lions in the April 2009 NFL Draft. Chris and I were determined to play with him in the NFL next year. My game plan was for us both to come out after this 2009 season—Chris as a senior and me as a junior. The writing was on the wall that I was going to be a first- or second-round draft pick. My coaches were telling me I was going to get ten passes a game thrown to me and some deep routes, too. I was excited as could be.

My goal was to be a top-ten pick and after that final spring game I was on a direct course to get there. I had watched tight ends Jeremy Shockey and Kellen Winslow play football in college and in the NFL. I liked that they played the game with toughness and determination and made the big catch. They both came out as juniors and were first-round picks, too.

Since I had such a high rating going into the year, and even though I was only a true junior, my dad wanted me to take out a disability insurance policy for $4 million, which was the maximum we could get. I knew better than to second-guess my dad when it came to business, so I took his advice and appreciated his buying that policy for me.

Coming off the best spring I ever had physically, I couldn't have been more confident. After spring practice ended in April, I didn't want to lose any momentum so I lifted weights in the gym with Chris like a madman. One day in April, the guys in the gym were all doing dead lifts, which is where the bar is loaded with heavy weight on each side and is on the floor. The idea is to start in a squatting position and then lift the bar to your hips, to where your back is straight upward in a standing position, and then lower the bar back down. I had never done dead lifts before as part of my training but one of the team strength trainers was supervising it, so I figured, why not? I should have paced myself and stayed at lighter weights but I got all macho, maxed it out, and went too heavy.

On the last set, I felt something pop in my back and it didn't feel right, but I finished lifting through the pain. I didn't think anything of it. I kept lifting and running all through April and May. It seemed like the harder I worked, the better it would feel that night. So the more it hurt, the harder I worked. Again I would feel great at night and then the next day it would hurt worse. I didn't say anything to anyone about it. I thought it would be temporary, that I could work through it and it would go away, but it didn't. The pain got progressively worse.

By July I had mad back pain. I felt shooting pains running down my legs. At the end of the month, it got so bad that the nerves in my legs weren't working. My legs felt like they weighed five hundred pounds each and I couldn't jump or run. It got to the point where I could barely feel my legs, so by the end of July, I finally told my dad and trainers.

We immediately got an MRI done on my back, which showed a badly ruptured disk that was damaging the nerves in my spinal cord. I got a first, second, and third opinion on my back. Dr. Robert Watkins, a specialist out of California, was the most renowned back doctor, and after talking with my dad at length, he laid out a two-step approach for me. First I would try physical therapy to rehab it. If that didn't work, I would have surgery to remove the part of the disk that was sticking out into the nerves in my spinal cord. I lost feeling in my legs because I had nerve damage and the concern was that I would not be able to regenerate the nerves to make a full recovery. If the nerves would not heal up from the damage, then I would have permanent damage to my legs. I couldn't believe it had gotten this bad.

I had always been able to get out of trouble in the past. When I was in the eighth grade, I was riding our brand-new four-wheeler and racing Chris. I turned too fast and wiped out going 30 miles per hour. The four-wheeler smashed into a tree, and I was sent flying over the handlebars and into another tree. The front of the four-wheeler was banged up pretty good. Chris's friend was there and tied a rope to it and helped us get it back home before our parents could see. I had a bad gash in my thigh but brushed it off. After a few days, though, the scab was getting worse and bigger. I was worried about getting into trouble so I didn't say anything. I didn't want to be the one who ruined it for everyone else if our parents took the four-wheelers away from us. So I went to football practice and hoped it would get better. It didn't, and after practice it was hurting until I pulled a three-inch-long piece of wood out of my leg. I was fine afterward and never got into trouble over it, but I learned my lesson and never took a turn that fast again. I should have learned another lesson: when you're injured, you have to address it.

I didn't address my back until it was too late and the damage was done. Now I had to hope that by working crazy hard in rehab, I could fix my back in time to play that season. I had a month to get my back and legs working again at full speed. If the physical therapy didn't work, I would have to have the surgery. There was another option, which was I could retire and collect $4 million tax-free at the age of nineteen. That's right, at any moment I could call it quits, do the rehab, and collect an IRS-proof check for $4 million . . . but I couldn't play football anymore. I did the math and at 4 percent annual interest per year, I could make $160,000 each year without touching the $4 million. That would be equivalent to me earning around $8 million before taxes in the NFL to break even.

The truth is, I didn't want the easy money. I wanted to earn it playing football. Maybe a lot of people would take the money and run, but I looked at it as quitting. I was happy playing football and didn't want to give that up. So I decided to try physical therapy. It was a long shot, but I had to try.

I was very lucky to have Randy Cohen as my trainer at the school to work with me. He talked with Dr. Watkins at length so they were both on the same page and they put together a specialized physical therapy rehab plan for me. Randy worked with me like it was his own back on the line. He got with me every day and helped me get better. The therapy was working. The pain in my back and the numbness in my legs started going away. I felt stronger and faster each day. I wasn't close to the point of being back to where I was before the injury, but I was improving and could start running. My goal was to be able to come back and play by midseason.

That second week of practice during the season, I tried to run routes and see if I was ready to start practicing. I felt good during the running but later that night, the shooting pains down my legs and the numbness all came back. I knew lying in my bed in the middle of the night, in pain that made me sweat right through my bedsheets, that my season was done. I knew I had no choice but to get the surgery. It was a horrible night for me. I kept thinking about how my oldest brother, Gord, had a bad back injury in college that prevented him from playing in the majors. I thought about how my dad's football career had been ruined by injuries. And now it was my turn to deal with injuries. My football career was in big trouble.

I flew out to California with my dad and had the surgery. Dr. Watkins explained to me that my legs were getting weaker because the disk had ruptured and the parts of it that broke off were pressing against the nerves in the spinal cord, causing nerve damage. The size of the broken-off disk particle was about an inch and the spinal canal area was two inches wide, so it was impacted pretty good. The procedure was for Dr. Watkins to use an instrument like a small pair of tweezers to poke a small hole through the ruptured disk, grab the broken-off part of the disk, and fish it out. The key was to make sure all the broken-off disk parts in the spinal canal were removed, that the hole in the disk closed up, and that the disk did not break off any more particles into the canal. So the disk had to stay intact; the spinal canal needs to be clear and nothing is supposed to touch nerves. The scary part was that even if all that happened and the surgery were a success, the nerve damage would have to reverse itself and the nerves would need to regenerate to the point they were before the damage took place. If the nerves didn't heal all the way back, then I would have permanent nerve damage and lose full use of my legs.

Dr. Watkins told me that this would be a team effort. He said that he could do the greatest surgery of all time but if my trainer didn't follow the special rehab program he designed for me and if I didn't work at it like I was supposed to do, then my football career would be over anyway. He made it very clear that I had to do the exercises in perfect form. That meant focusing mentally on doing it exactly like I was told to do it and busting my butt physically to give it my best effort each and every time.

I was lucky that my whole life I had been trained to understand the importance of perfect technique. When we had the weight lifting equipment in our basement, my dad taught us to pay attention and use the right form or else we would hurt ourselves. When my dad took us to Demeris Johnson for training, Demeris drilled it into our heads that we had to run properly and do the drills exactly like he showed us. My high school coach Mammo taught me about using technique to block and tackle. My college coaches taught me that I had to use technique to get off the jam and get separation on routes. I learned the hard way that to block big, fast defensive ends at the college level, technique was critical, just like it is with wrestling. So my whole life I was trained to take instructions and do things properly every time. My dad instilled in all of us the mentality of being trained to win. It was now up to me to use that training to get my back healthy.

The worst part for me was the first three weeks after surgery, a period when I couldn't do anything but walk to class and sit in a recliner. I couldn't get comfortable, and going to class was not fun. I couldn't turn or bend. I was fragile and every wrong move sent sharp pain up my spine and down my legs. The simplest of things that I took for granted, like being able to go to the bathroom or brush my teeth, were very difficult. My body felt so heavy, like I was tied down. I wanted to get up and move around but I had to stay disciplined and just sit in the recliner. My brother and the rest of my teammates were playing football and having the time of their lives, while I was anchored to that chair. That was a real low point for me, because there was nothing I could do to get better but wait until I could begin my rehab. The game that I love was taken away from me. It pissed me off not to be out there playing on the field with my teammates. I was supposed to be the man, the best tight end in college football. Instead I was sitting in a recliner facing the fact that I might never have full use of my legs again no matter how hard I tried.

Sitting there every night, not able to party, not having fun, not getting wild, could have easily gotten the best of me, but I wouldn't let myself get down. I went through the mono thing the previous year and got through that better than ever and I kept telling myself I would beat this, too. I refused to be afraid that my legs wouldn't come back to being strong and fast like they were. I blocked it out and didn't focus on the fear or negatives. I focused on the positives, including the fact that after six weeks I could start doing back and core exercises.

Though I stayed as positive as I could those six weeks and didn't fall off the deep end, I was still in a miserable funk and couldn't wait to get off that recliner. Once the six-week mark came, I couldn't wait to start doing my exercises with Randy. All I wanted to do was get to work. I was doing planks, supermans, and all kinds of exercises where I was on all fours lifting my legs and arms. Being able to exercise fueled my positive energy, and my fun-loving personality was in full swing.

I think it's because I'm such a big kid at heart and always joking around that I am able to keep the pressure from getting to me. I just laugh it off and keep working. There's no reason you can't work hard, do what you are supposed to, and still have fun in the process. So when it's time to pay attention and go hard, that's what I do. Before, after, and in between is when I have fun. It keeps me positive, ready for more work instead of getting burnt out.

I was so happy to be off that recliner and doing any type of exercise that I was hyped up to do whatever core and back exercises Randy told me to do. What was super-helpful was that Randy would show me the exact form, and from there I focused on doing it exactly the way he showed me. I kept thinking about what Dr. Watkins told me, that the success of the surgery would be up to me and Randy with the rehab. To Randy's credit, he worked with me like I was the star player getting ready for the big game this week even though everyone knew I was done for the season and maybe forever. At some schools, they kind of forget about you and treat you like a second-class citizen once you are out for the year—that wasn't the case at Arizona. Randy was a first-class trainer and person.

This time, I wasn't working hard for fun or to be the best. This time I was working to save my career and regain the full use of my legs. I looked at it like my whole life I had been preparing for this challenge, only I just didn't know it until I was faced with the biggest fight of my life. I learned from my dad that everyone works hard but the winners are the ones who are trained to pay attention to the details and perfect all the little things. With my career on the line, I focused on understanding every tiny detail of my technique in every single exercise I did. That is the mentality of a professional. That is the difference between being trained and untrained.

Armed with that training, I was able to stay upbeat, work as hard as I could mentally and physically, and begin to make progress. Each day I got closer to my goal of getting back on the field and each day I had more and more positive energy. I was getting hyped up and having fun again but I did it smart. I didn't goof around and risk getting hurt.

After eight weeks, in mid-November, I was able to start jogging and do light weight lifting. By mid-December I was doing light running and was progressing. I felt good and like myself again. I now had a hard decision to make and three options to choose from—retire, stay in school for my 2010 senior year, or enter the 2010 NFL Draft early as a junior.

The key was that my tax-free $4 million insurance policy gave me until the third game of the 2010 college season to retire and collect the money. If I were to stay in school for my senior year, I would continue the rehab, and by the third game of the season in September I would have to retire and give up football or play my senior year out and give up the policy. So if I retired before the third game, I could collect on the policy, get my college degree, and be set for life. If I played past my third game in college and then reinjured my back, I would get nothing. On the other hand, if I stayed healthy, I could get my college degree and then go play in the NFL in 2011. Again, if I stayed in school for 2010 and then reinjured my back after the third game, I wouldn't get the insurance money, my football career would be over, and I'd risk permanent nerve damage. My third option was to immediately start training for the NFL Combine (which was in February 2010) and if the training went well, I could enter the NFL Draft. If my training didn't go well, I could still go back to Arizona and play college football. The key to my third option was that I had to make the decision by January 15, which is the deadline for college juniors to declare for the NFL Draft. Once you declare for the draft by January 15, you give up your college eligibility and can't go back to play college football.

But before I could make any decision, I had a major hurdle to clear. I needed to get reexamined and get clearance from Dr. Watkins to play football again. There were a bunch of concerns. First, we had to make sure there were no further disk parts that broke off into the spinal canal and caused more nerve damage. The second concern was that the spinal canal needed to be intact and not narrowing. The third concern was that the nerve damage could be partially permanent and not regenerate. Dr. Watkins could address only the first two concerns. Only time would tell about the nerve regeneration. While I was waiting on Dr. Watkins to let us know the results, I was very optimistic. I just believed in my body, that it would come through for me.

Great news! Dr. Watkins said my disk had healed perfectly and there were no more fragments in the spinal canal. I was happy but not surprised.

That's right, I was back! Having my ability to play the game that I love taken away from me made me appreciate football and being part of a team that much more. I lost my junior year of football, I lost my strength, my feeling of invincibility, but not my confidence and sense of humor. I admit, it hurt not to be part of the team, not to be on the field and having fun with the guys. I was happy for Chris and my teammates when they won, but I wasn't able to party, to celebrate and get wild and go crazy having fun like I was used to doing. I couldn't enjoy the experience of college life, and thought about how tough it must have been for my dad to deal with his injuries and have to move on. I was lucky: I had Dr. Watkins and a great trainer to help me. Everything I had gone through had made me tougher and more determined to play football again. And getting the green light from Dr. Watkins made me rev my engines and put the pedal to the metal.

8

THE GRONK AGENT SELECTION METHOD

I was determined to live the life of an NFL player rather than be someone who quit and took the easy insurance money. I believed one hundred percent that I would make it all the way back. I was lightly running and lifting, feeling good, but I was nowhere close to being strong, agile, or fast. Although I had come so far, I still had a long way to go and only one month to get there since I had until the January 15, 2010, deadline to make my final decision. If my training continued to progress and I had a fair chance for a strong recovery, then I was going to declare for the NFL. If I came out and played in the NFL, I would be forfeiting my $4 million tax-free insurance money. On the flip side, if my training didn't show enough progress, then I would have to stay in school and see if I could play football by the third college game. If the answer was yes, I would give up the insurance money. If I couldn't get back to full health or close enough to it by the third college game, then I never would make it back and at least I would have the insurance money to fall back on. But I blocked this last part out of my mind.

That month of training from December 15 to January 15 would be critical to my chances of playing in the NFL, so I went to one of the top NFL Combine trainers, Pete Bommarito. The year before, my brother Dan had to pick a trainer to prepare for the NFL Combine. The NFL Combine takes place in February at Indianapolis and is the event where the top players entering the April NFL Draft are flown in by the NFL to do medical exams and interviews and perform various speed and agility drills. My dad, being in the fitness industry and having the ear of several top NFL executives he could trust, did his homework on the top trainers for the NFL and thoroughly checked them out. In the end, he picked Pete Bommarito out of Miami, Florida, to train Dan. Dan had awesome results at the NFL Combine and Pete proved he was legit. With my family having firsthand experience with Pete, it was a no-brainer for me to train with him. Normally an agent pays for the training, but since I could not have an agent until I made my decision on January 15 (signing with an agent would cancel my college eligibility), my dad paid Pete out of his own pocket.

I had another decision to make as well: picking an agent. If I was going to come out for the NFL, I would want to hit the ground running with an agent in place on January 15. Dan had an agent who did a solid job for him and Chris knew an agent he liked, but I wanted to go with whoever I thought was the best fit for me. Both Dan and Chris were in the same boat. They were not expected to be high draft picks and it made sense for them to go with smaller-firm agents who could focus on them. As for me, I wanted to go with the number-one agent in the country. I figured that if I was the best tight end, I should have the best agent.

Word got out that we were talking to agents and I was flooded with phone calls from them. I told them all to talk with my dad. He would screen them, narrow it down, and then set up meetings with the final group of agents he thought would be the best for me. From there, I would make the final call.

We invited several agents to come to our house in Arizona to meet me, Chris, and my mom and dad. Everybody was impressive and they all had their own sales pitches, but by the end of the meeting I wasn't fired up about anybody. The one thing they all had in common was that they bad-mouthed the same agent—Drew Rosenhaus. They called him every dirty name in the book . . . you name it, they used it to describe him.

Despite all the bad stuff the other agents said, my dad agreed to have the meeting with Drew, and for three reasons: 1) the NFL general managers and coaches that my dad knew spoke very highly of Drew as an agent; 2) we wanted to be thorough and give Drew a fair shot to address the name-calling; and 3) we wanted to see for ourselves who this guy was that the other agents hated so much.

Drew showed up with his brother Jason and they were wearing blue jeans, sneakers, and their company T-shirts. I was in shorts and a T-shirt as well but my parents were dressed for business.

Drew made conversation with me right away about this and that, but not business. He came across as funny and smooth. Jason was more serious. When it came time to talk business, Drew pretty much focused on my dad the whole time.

My dad is a big guy who can be really scary and intimidating, or really fun and friendly. With Drew and Jason my dad was very intense and went for their throats. I thought it would be fun to watch my dad go to work on Drew, since he had worked over the other agents pretty good on their weak points. As I said, Dad knew the inside scoop on every agent we met with because a couple of GMs and coaches had given my dad their scouting report on them. So my dad wanted to test each agent and see how they held up under fire. So he let Drew and Jason get into their presentations first.

When Drew was still making small talk with me, my dad interrupted him and said, "Let's get down to business. Show us why Rob should hire you guys."

Drew went right to work and showed us who his clients were. He pointed out that earlier in his career, he represented Pro Bowl tight ends Jeremy Shockey, Kellen Winslow, first-rounder Greg Olsen, first-rounder Benjamin Watson, and several other good tight ends, including Eric Green and Randy McMichael. They showed us charts on all the tight end contracts that he and Jason had negotiated over the past ten years. They showed us a list of all the juniors they represented over the years. Drew pointed out that Jeremy Shockey, Kellen Winslow, and Greg Olsen all came out as juniors and went in the first round.

Drew said he had represented running back Willis McGahee, who went in the first round of the 2003 Draft even though he was coming off a severe injury, just like I was. Drew also pointed out that he represented two former University of Arizona players who were now Pro Bowlers: linebackers Lance Briggs and Antonio Pierce. Then Jason took us through chart after chart about their tight end, rookie, and free agent contracts, and they were impressive. The charts showed a head-to-head matchup of their contracts versus the competition's, and theirs looked better. These guys were confident and convincing. They backed up the tough talk.

Then Drew challenged me. He said, "Okay, Rob, name any team you want, and I'll tell you all about their tight ends. Pick any team you want. . . ."

So I named the Buffalo Bills and he took me through their starter and backups, where they went to school, how long they'd been in the NFL, what they were making, etc. Drew then took me through the tight end situation for every team in the league. I was impressed. These guys had experience with tight ends, with juniors, and with injured rookies. They seemed like a perfect fit for me, but we were all still wondering about one thing. Finally my dad brought it up.

My dad looked Drew in the eye and with a tough look said, "Drew, this is impressive and I've heard from the teams that you're a top agent. But tell me, why is it all the other agents call you a —sucker, a f—in' —hole, a crook, a dirtbag . . . ? What's their problem with you?" Even I was shocked that my dad didn't hold back.

Drew immediately answered right back, "Great question!

Thanks for asking, and I'll tell you why they're all gunning for me. It's because I'm the best in the business and I keep kicking their butts! I'm perfectly suited to work for you guys and they know that. They all know I'm the guy that everybody needs to beat. I have the better contracts, the better track record, the better clients, and I outwork all of them. They can't compete with me and Jason. All they can do is talk smack behind our back. You didn't see me mention any other agent's name and you won't. I'm here to talk about myself. About what I can do for your family because I'm the best in the business and your son is the best tight end in the country. He should have an agent that will fight for him, talk directly to the GMs, and make sure they know that Rob's back is healthy, that he's the best tight end in the draft by far and it would be a huge mistake not to take him because of it. . . ."

Drew had an answer for everything. He was fired up, fearless, and ready to fight for me—that's what I wanted. My dad liked him, too. Since my dad was the top guy in his own business, his competitors all bad-mouthed him, too, so he understood. The decision came down to Drew and Jason versus a smaller agent that Chris and I both liked. I put the decision off until January 15 to see if I was going to need an agent or stay in school. If the medical report came back negative, I wouldn't need an agent.

It was time to work harder than I had ever done in my life. I started training with Pete in Miami in mid-December. My dad was on the phone with Pete every day getting a progress report. It would be up to Pete to determine if I could be ready to work out for teams at a high level in March, or if I needed to go back to school and give it until September. Pete worked me from 6 a.m. until 7 p.m. every day. I was constantly doing something, whether it was pool work, light jogging, light lifting, working on the treadmill, getting a massage, getting electrical treatments, or getting all kinds of specialized therapy that Pete threw at me.

Whatever it was they asked me to do, I did exactly that, each time with maximum effort. I was always on time and never missed a session. I ate the foods Pete had prepared for me and went to bed when he said. But thank God I had Chris with me. He kept it fun and helped me get through the frustration of being behind while everyone was healthy and running at full speed. With Chris there, we were always joking around and keeping it light. The only time the scary thoughts got in my head was at night but by then I was too exhausted to do anything but sleep.

Pete explained to me that I had a huge football player's body and I was being trained to run like a track athlete with a smaller body. He got pretty technical with me but the gist of it is that you can do super-intense work, where you push the soft tissue of your body, for only a limited amount of reps. If you go extremely hard too much, it backfires. You can't waste those reps, because if you have to redo them or don't do them right, you can tear muscles, ligaments, or tendons. I couldn't afford any setbacks. I had to protect my soft tissue from injury, especially in my back and legs, and the only way to do that was to go at the maximum when I was supposed to go hard. Most of the time is downtime, with lighter work to let your body heal up and recover, so when it is go-time you have to go all the way, the right way, on every limited rep you get.

Dr. Watkins explained to me that the success of getting my legs back to full speed would depend on how hard I worked and followed instructions. After that, I became a straight-A student at rehabbing my back and legs. I trusted in Dr. Watkins, Randy Cohen, and Pete Bommarito. I trusted in my ability to take in everything they told me and apply it. I trusted in my willpower to heal my body. As a result, Pete told us on January 13 that it was his professional opinion that I would be able to make a good enough recovery to reach the average level of athleticism for an NFL tight end. He said there was a decent chance I could make it all the way back to above-average athleticism for an NFL tight end.

That was all I needed to hear—that I had a shot to make it all the way back. I knew all along that I didn't want the insurance money, that I wanted to be an NFL player and live that life to the fullest. I didn't hesitate when I made the decision to come out, to turn down the $4 million in insurance money and enter the 2010 NFL Draft.

Once I made my decision, I had to meet with my head coach, Mike Stoops, at Arizona and let him know. He, Coach Dimel, and everyone else at Arizona had been very positive and supportive of me during my rehab. A lot of college head coaches care only about what's best for them and do everything they can to get juniors to stay in school regardless of what is best for the player. Not Coach Stoops. I'm sure it would have been great for him if I had come back and played on his team that 2010 season. He made some good points for why I should consider staying but I didn't want to risk getting hurt again and missing out on my chance to play in the NFL. Coach understood that, respected my decision, and supported me all the way. He was a class act.

Now I needed to get my agent in place. I wanted someone aggressive and hardworking. I had busted my butt to get this far and wanted an agent who would do the same in marketing me to teams and getting me the best contract. My dad liked Drew because he said connections in business are very important and Drew is connected with the teams. One NFL general manager told my dad that if it were his own son, he would want him with Drew. The GM said, "Sometimes I'm pissed at Drew because he pushes hard for more than I want to pay, but in the end we always get the deal done and it's a good deal for both sides."

Drew wasn't one of the agents who tried to give me money under the table while I was still in school. He was on the level, and I was leaning toward Drew. On the other hand, I did like another agent a lot, too. He was brash and cocky like Drew. He was not as experienced as Drew but he wasn't a rookie, either. He promised me he would work all day, every day on me as his client and give me more personal attention than Drew or Jason could. Our personalities really clicked and Chris wanted to go with him, too, so I was torn. Chris thought Drew would be too busy to focus on Chris as much as the other agent could. I liked the idea of Chris and me having the same agent, to keep it in the family, so I was on the fence.

Knowing I had to make a final decision fast, I set up a final meeting in Miami. I met with Chris's guy first and was very comfortable going with him. Then I had Drew and Jason come over to my condo. Drew did most of the talking and got loud; he talked in my face and got me fired up. I didn't know it at the time, but Chris was with the other agent in the unit next door. Next thing I knew, the other agent barged in and interrupted the meeting.

Chris must have put him up to it.

When the agent walked in, Drew said to him very politely, "Excuse me. Do you mind? You've had your turn to meet with Rob; now it's my turn. I'd appreciate you showing me some professional courtesy and allow me to finish my meeting." Then Jason said, "We just got started here. Let us finish our meeting and then come back after."

He said, "If Rob wants me to stay, I'm staying."

They all looked at me and I didn't know what to say, so I was like, "Yeah, whatever, if you want to stay, you can stay." I didn't mind seeing my top two finalists compete.

Drew went back to making his points, ignoring the agent who was in the kitchen area with Chris while we were in the living room. Every time Drew would say something, Chris would ask the agent, "What do you think?" The agent would have a smart-aleck remark and we liked it. The agent was cocky and kept interrupting with his snide remarks.

It didn't take long for Drew to get up and say, "Okay, if you are going to interrupt me and talk, then let's go back and forth."

Drew just attacked: "How many clients do you have? How many tight ends do you represent? Here's how many I have. How about you?"

Then Jason jumped in: "How many first-round picks do you

represent? How many millions of dollars did you negotiate this year? How many true juniors have you represented in the draft?"

Then Drew went at him again: "How many injured players in the draft have you represented? How many players from Arizona? How many Pro Bowl players do you have? How many fifty-million-dollar contracts have you negotiated? I've negotiated more contracts this past year than you have in your entire career."

The other agent didn't have anything to say other than "You're unprofessional, you're arrogant, you're always in the media. I have a life. I'm not a dirtbag. . . ."

That was it. Drew walked into the kitchen and got in his face: "You shouldn't be here interrupting my meeting. I'm having a professional debate with you and you are making it personal, not professional. You're insulting me, calling me names. I've had enough. You want to get personal? You want to interfere? Okay, f—k you! You're a coward! You're a disgrace to this business. You p—y! Let's go right here, right now! You b—h! I'll give you the first shot."

The other agent was shaking with anger, he had an ugly look on his reddened face and his hand was balled up into a fist. Chris and I were loving it. This was ugly and was going to come to blows!

The agent bit his lip and said, "Not gonna happen!" Then he walked out the door.

Drew apologized to me for getting unprofessional and then Chris asked him and Jason to leave, which they did. Now, Chris had had my dad listening on the phone the whole time as the agents went back and forth. I grabbed the phone and told my dad, "I'm going with Drew!"

Having my two top choices go head-to-head and see who would argue the best and fight the hardest for me was the perfect way for me to see for myself who would do the same for me with the teams. Not a bad way to pick your agent.

I had my agent in place and my training was on track. Now I just needed to get my legs at full power.

9

THE GRONKS ARE COMING TO TOWN!

I knew all along that I would not be ready to work out at the 2010 NFL Combine in Indianapolis in February. I didn't go there to work out. I went there so that the teams could do their medical exams on my back and see for themselves how I was doing. I had not run full speed yet but I was ready to start trying. The first two days were taken up with a lengthy physical, MRI exams, X-rays, and tons of interviews with teams. I measured in at 6′6″, 258 pounds. I wasn't able to do any of the drills, like a forty-yard dash, vertical leap, standing broad jump, or routes. The only thing I was able to do was bench-press. I put up twenty-three reps, which was a solid performance considering I have long arms, which makes benching more challenging. Guys with short arms have an easier time benching.

It felt good to bench at least, but it was frustrating not to run and do everything else that all the guys were doing. I wanted to compete and show them I was the best, but I wasn't ready. All I could do was go to meetings with individual teams, which pretty much all asked me the same questions. Most teams wanted to know how my back was and if I was a party animal at college. I told them the truth, that my back was doing awesome. As far as the partying goes, I said that though I was a party rocker in college, I didn't do much during the season, and work always came first. I shot them straight because they knew the truth anyway. They just wanted to see if I would lie about it or be honest. No one's perfect and everyone has their fair share of skeletons in the closet, but I had nothing major to hide or be ashamed of.

I'm no Boy Scout, I'm a Gronk. When my dad and Gord went to my opening game with Chris for Arizona, it was at BYU. Now, we had all gone to plenty of Dan's games at Maryland, where there was a college partying atmosphere in the crowd. When they went to BYU, they did not fit in. My family was wearing Arizona gear and beads and was proudly strutting their colors. Every BYU fan they met was courteous, polite, and friendly, not drunk and obnoxious. They were wishing good luck to my dad and offering food from their tailgating parties. Supernice people. There was no drinking beer in that stadium; it was football, religious-oriented fun, and a family atmosphere. The Gronks stand out in a place like that because we are going to have a few beers, be loud, lose some shirts, and get crazy. But we don't start trouble with anyone, and we don't talk smack about the other team; we just cheer our guys on, keep to ourselves, and have a great time.

So when I met with all the GMs and coaches, I wasn't going to portray myself as some super-clean-cut, ultraconservative religious guy—that's not me. Teams knew I was wild but also that I kept it in check. Remember, most of the coaches and executives had been wild college football players in their younger days, too.

The teams told me and Drew that where I would be drafted would depend on how well I worked out at my University of Arizona Pro Day on March 27. The Pro Day is the workout I (and my other teammates coming out for the draft) have at my school, where the interested NFL teams come to watch me run the forty-yard dash and all the other drills I wasn't ready to do at the Combine. As soon as I got back from the Combine in late February, it was time for me to start running full speed and go all-out. So I did a mock Combine performance and couldn't believe how badly I did. I ran a 5.0 forty-yard dash, which was embarrassing, and on the standing broad jump I did only seven feet. I was shocked.

Oh man! Did I blow it? I asked myself. I couldn't help but have those doubts. I had never looked that bad in my life before. I was stiff, slow, heavy, and late in my movements. I had one month until my personal workout at the Pro Day, and if I didn't improve, I wasn't gonna get drafted. I knew I was in trouble. I had trained all that time since the surgery and here I was in late February running and jumping like someone who didn't belong on the field. Maybe I had made a huge mistake. Maybe my legs weren't going to make it back to where I was. Maybe I should have stayed in school and taken the insurance money. I heard a lot of maybes in my head but going back was not an option. All I could do was move forward.

I could have panicked and gotten upset but I didn't. I watched the video of my forty and my routes and all the drills. I watched how I wasn't bending, leaning, and using the technique from head to toe that I needed to use. I went over it and over it in my mind. I drilled, drilled, and drilled some more. I did all my exercises and therapy sessions. I have to admit that $4 million in insurance money was in the back of my mind, but I didn't let it get to me. I just stayed with the program of eating my meals, doing my drills, perfecting every single detail of my footwork, hips, shoulders, and hand movements. I just lived, ate, and breathed my training program.

I didn't run another forty again until one week before my Arizona workout. I did another mock Combine and this time I was a new man. I felt fast, explosive, and strong and had my feet under me. I felt like myself again. It was only a few weeks later, but my feet felt light and quick. I could stick my foot in the ground to plant and accelerate in my routes. I was too winded to scream with excitement, but inside I was partying.

So on March 27, 2010, I had a full workout at my school for NFL teams. I felt confident and had my technique down perfectly. I ran my forty and nailed it. The NFL teams clocked me at a 4.63, which made a definite statement that I was one hundred percent back. Yeah, baby! Let's go! That's what I'm talking about!

I ran what seemed like a million routes and was too tired to show how fired up I was, but that's what I was thinking. I was hoping for a mid-4.7 and was beyond crazy when I heard that time. I jumped 9'11" on my broad jump and my vertical was 33½ inches. I had really made it back. Thanks to the support of my parents, Chris, Dr. Watkins, Randy Cohen, and Pete, my Pro Day performance made the decision to come out the right one. All that hard work to rehab my back had paid off. I was ready for the draft.

In the meantime I made a lot of visits to NFL teams. They would fly me in to their facilities and meet with me to go over film and test my general football IQ. I had excellent visits with the Baltimore Ravens, Denver Broncos, Miami Dolphins, and New England Patriots. Those were the teams that we thought would draft me in the first or second round.

The 2010 draft was the NFL's seventy-fifth and took place at Radio City Music Hall in New York City. The league put me and my family up in a sweet hotel room. The game plan was for Jason Rosenhaus to be in position with us Thursday night if I got the call in the first round. If not, Drew would fly in Friday to take over. Jason met up with us in the hotel suite shortly before we were supposed to head down there. When he knocked on the door, my dad let him in. My mom tried to apologize in advance and prepare him for the scene, but Jason walked in in his suit and tie only to see me, Gord, Dan, and Glenn ("Goose")—all four of us—on the big bed just wrestling with each other. Across from the bed, the bathroom door was open—with Chris sitting on the throne.

"I take it you guys need a few more minutes to get ready," Jason said with a laugh. Even a fancy hotel room in the Big Apple wasn't going to slow down the Gronks.

The draft format had been changed that year. For the first time, the first round would be Thursday night, the second and third rounds would be Friday night, and the fourth through seventh rounds would be held on Saturday afternoon. I knew I was going to go either in the mid-to-late first or the early-to-mid second round. There are thirty-two picks in each round and the first round gives each team ten minutes to make their pick one after another.

There were about thirty players there at the draft and each had his own table where he sat with his agent and family. I knew that it would be a close call as to whether I got drafted Thursday night in the first round, and I prepared myself as best as I could in case I was drafted in the second round. Still, I'm a competitor. I knew I was one of the best players in the draft, period. I recognized the fact that I had missed my entire junior year because of the injury, and that that was an issue for some teams, but I was confident that whoever drafted me wouldn't regret it.

We—me, my parents, my brothers, and Jason—sat there patiently at our table for the first couple of hours. Then they got to the twenty-first pick. The Bengals had it and we knew they weren't going to take me because they liked the other tight end, Jermaine Gresham, out of Oklahoma, more. What I wanted was for the Bengals to take Gresham so I would be the next tight end taken. They indeed took him and now anything could happen.

The Broncos had the twenty-second pick and liked me. I knew

Denver was a possibility but my cell phone didn't ring, and they took wide receiver Demaryius Thomas instead. The Broncos also had the twenty-fifth pick and took Tim Tebow, which was a double bummer: now I definitely wasn't going to the Broncos, plus they had traded picks with the Ravens, who were now out of the first round.

The Patriots were up next, and the Dolphins after that, but both teams picked defensive players instead of me. I was surprised New England didn't take me. Drew and Coach Bill Belichick had communicated several times about taking me and I thought offensive coordinator Bill O'Brien (now the Houston Texans head coach) really liked me. I sat there that night and felt rejected. My mom will tell you it was one of the few times she ever saw me in a bad mood.

None of the NFL teams thought I was good enough for the first round? I told myself that as long as I went in the second round, I'd be okay, but I was still pissed off. I had wanted to go in the first round not because of the money, but because of the respect: because that's where the best players are supposed to get picked. Jason told us at the table that while it might be more prestigious and exciting to go in the first round, it can be better to be an early second-rounder than a late first because second-round picks sign four-year deals and first-rounders sign five-year deals. The shorter deal makes it a lot easier to get an extension early on than is the case if you have a five-year deal, and the real money is in that second contract. Jason said being a second-round pick also still gets you a nice signing bonus.

It made sense, sure, but I was mad at the NFL and my emotions got more and more intense. I didn't sleep well that night and the next day, Friday, waited for the draft to get going that night. The Dolphins at no. 8, the Bills at no. 9, and the Ravens at no. 11 were the best options to go at the top of round two. The Dolphins and my hometown Bills passed at no. 8 and no. 9. My next hope was the Ravens at no. 11. Then my cell phone rang and it was the Patriots on the line. The Raiders were on the clock at no. 10, so I didn't know why the Pats were calling. It turned out that yes, the Raiders had the pick, but the Patriots were trading up to get me. With a rush of emotion, I instantly thought about playing with future Hall of Fame quarterback Tom Brady on a Super Bowl–caliber team, with one of the best coaches ever in Bill Belichick. I had really liked their offensive coordinator, Coach O'Brien, too, and wanted so much to be on a winning team.

I couldn't really speak. I was as emotional as I've ever been in my life. I got off the phone and stood up, then my dad brought us all into a huddle. I gave him and my mom huge hugs and held back tears. Then Commissioner Roger Goodell said, "With the forty-second pick in the 2010 NFL Draft, the New England Patriots select Rob Gronkowski, tight end, Arizona."

We went wild and all hugged each other. I took the podium, put on my Patriot cap, then grabbed a Patriot helmet. After I thanked the commissioner, Deion Sanders interviewed me onstage and I told him, "This is the greatest moment of my life. This is unbelievable." I was holding back tears as I talked. I was so happy. My family and I were overwhelmed. I had been through so much, missing this past year and almost having the game taken away from me. Now I was a New England Patriot!

We formed a huddle again and chest-bumped each other. I put the helmet on and screamed at the top of my lungs at the TV camera. We hooted and hollered until the Patriots called back and told me to get offstage. Right then and there we let the NFL and the Patriots know, you'd better watch out! The Gronks are coming to town and we are going to bring it!

10

WELCOME TO THE NFL

About a week after the draft, I went to the Patriots facility in Foxborough, Massachusetts, for the May rookie minicamp. Just the rookies were there, so I didn't get to meet Tom Brady yet. When we got there, Coach Belichick told us right off the bat that it didn't matter if you were a first-round pick or an undrafted free agent: everyone seated in a chair would be treated the same. He told us that if we worked hard, knew our plays, and took advantage of our opportunity, then we would get more opportunities. If we didn't, then he'd replace us with someone who would. He talked to us straight; he told us everyone gets a fair shot and he treated us like professionals. He made me want to get to work.

A few weeks later we had a full-team minicamp. The camp was

in the middle of nowhere so it was easy to focus just on working. To be healthy, to be pain-free, to be strong, light on my feet, and feel fast were superexciting for me. I just studied my playbook; I didn't go out. I tried to fit in, stayed humble, and soaked in what the other guys were doing, like a sponge.

When the veterans got there, I eagerly got to the facility first thing in the morning. I went into the training room to get my ankles taped so I could take the field nice and early. While I was getting taped, Tom Brady, the legendary quarterback that I had been watching on TV since middle school, actually introduced himself to me: "Hey, I'm Tom Brady, nice to meet you."

"What's up! I'm Rob." I didn't really know what to say other than that. Being a rookie, I was intimidated and didn't want to say the wrong thing. I had all the respect in the world for him and did not want to get on his wrong side. It was a brief introduction, on the fly as he was walking through. I couldn't know it at the time, but that would end up pretty much the nicest he was to me over the entire year.

We all hit the field shortly after. I was watching Tom throw passes to the veteran receivers, and was waiting for my turn. I finally got to run the drill with him. It was the easiest route in the world, just run straight fifteen yards up the field and then turn around to catch it. I ran at 75 percent like I was told to do and turned around for the ball. I had run that drill a million times in my life and could catch that ball in my sleep. And yet from the moment I lined up to run and until I turned around, I couldn't stop telling myself, "You better catch that ball! Tom Brady is throwing you that ball and you need to catch it!"

That's the worst kind of thing that can happen to a receiver. You don't want to be thinking anything or feeling any pressure. You just want to let instinct take over and to do automatically what you are trained to do. This felt like life-or-death. But I made the catch, and you know what, I realized it was just like any other ball thrown to me. After that I felt a little better in practice and loosened up.

Then came training camp at the end of July. We finally got to put the pads on. Remember, I hadn't worn pads, blocked, or taken a hit in a long time. I was now in an NFL training camp, the New England Patriots', going up against world-class athletes and professional football players. The toughest part for me was not the physical matchups. It was learning the playbook, which is like a whole new language. And you have to know not only the plays, but also the adjustments Tom wants you to make on your route based on the defensive coverage. You have to see what he sees and think what he thinks. Now, Tom was a rookie in 2000 and here I was in 2010 being a rookie myself. I had tons to learn and no time to learn it in if I wanted to play. And it's not like Coach Belichick and Tom were going to say, "You know what, we are not going to run any specific play until you know it and are completely comfortable with it."

No way. They are going to run whatever play they want and I'd better know it or I won't be on the field. So the whole time, in the huddle and while I'm lining up and getting ready to block or run the route, I am thinking about what I am supposed to do, where

I am supposed to be, who I am supposed to block, what I am supposed to read in the defense, what Tom wants me to do . . .

I felt like a robot. I was struggling to make sure I was doing what I was supposed to do and then do it as fast as I could, as hard as I could, and with the best technique that I could. I've been playing football all my life. I know the game, I know how to play, but this was overwhelming. I studied and studied and studied that playbook. I wasn't going to piss off Tom Brady or Coach Belichick or our offensive coordinator, Bill O'Brien, who called the plays. Or so I thought.

I wasn't consistent in training camp. Some days I flashed real talent and other days I couldn't get any separation and looked unimpressive. The one thing that was consistent was my effort. I went hard over and over again. And along the way, I was taught a couple of lessons.

The veteran tight end who helped show me the ropes was Alge Crumpler. Alge was superstrong and known for being a beast of a blocker. On the very first blocking drill, I was supposed to run at half speed into a big pad (held by Alge), hit it with my hands, and drive him back. Well, I went and hit the pad but I didn't drive Alge backward. Alge braced for the hit, timed it just right, and used his massive body strength to knock me to my knees. I couldn't believe how strong he was. I was embarrassed and made sure not to underestimate him or any other blocker again.

With that in mind, I wanted to show my teammates I was a bad dude. The perfect opportunity to prove it came my way in practice when my assignment was to do a wham block against the nose tackle. A wham block is designed for me to come from the blind side of the defensive tackle and put my shoulder into him with my full weight and knock him on his butt before he sees me coming. This was my chance to make a statement and it was against Pro Bowl monster nose tackle Vince Wilfork, who was the biggest, baddest unmovable mountain in the NFL. Vince is five inches shorter and about a hundred pounds heavier than me. He is massive. This is one play no tight end wants to do but I was going to show everyone I was a fearless, crazy wild man to watch out for. So I went all-out, full speed right into Vince. Remember, the only chance you have against the bigger guy is to hit him off balance before he sees it coming.

Unfortunately for me, someone tipped off Vince that I was coming, so he was waiting on me. I could have sworn I saw him smiling when I came at him. That's when I knew I was in trouble. Me being who I am, I had no choice but to keep coming and take my beating like a man. Instead of me blindsiding and dropping him, he came after *me,* delivering a demolishing shoulder hit and knocking me five feet backward in the air. I don't know if that play was called to set me up, but I got my you-know-what handed to me. That was my welcome-to-the-NFL moment. Hello!

I felt that hit everywhere in my head and body. I got up and was never going to try that again, and never have to this day. The next time in practice, I gave Vince a little courtesy bump in the shoulder and he did the same back. There's a difference between being crazy and being stupid and I learned that lesson from Professor Wilfork.

After learning a lesson like that the hard way, I always picked myself up and kept at it like the Energizer Bunny. I got rep after rep after rep with the first team, second team, third team, and even when it was just the rookies. I was getting into great shape and it was a phenomenal on-the-job learning experience.

No more or no less than any other rookie, I occasionally didn't run the right route the right way and end up right where I was supposed to be. Every now and again, I didn't block the right guy using the right angle to block him toward the right direction. As with every rookie, it was a learning process. I had a high football IQ but there is a lot to learn and it took time to know it and then know it well at full speed. It takes practice and practice and more practice. I stayed after practice to work on my routes and doing the little things my coaches wanted. But once the pads came on, if I made a mistake, Tom would blast me. He was like a drill sergeant toward me. In the meeting rooms he was supertough on me. I thought he didn't like me. I would take it and keep my mouth shut because, first, he was Tom Brady; second, he was right; and third, I was a rookie who hadn't accomplished anything in the NFL.

One part of training camp was fun: the rookie hazing. During one hot practice, the vets took a hose and sprayed cold water on the grass to create a fifteen-yard slip-and-slide area. Given my days at Club G, this was right up my alley. All rookies had to do it only once. I did it three times and had a blast. We were in full pads and helmet. I went first and did it headfirst, then feetfirst, and then did all kinds of funny moves just being me. Each time I got a big running start and jumped full speed into it. The hazing aspect was that it took place right before practice started, so you got superdrenched and then it felt like you were carrying an extra fifty pounds on your back. They made me take a million reps in practice knowing I was soaked and weighed down. I didn't care.

In another initiation rite we rookies were gathered in front of the veterans for a players-only meeting. All of the rookies had to tell a funny story. When it was my turn, only one tale came to mind. In the spring after my freshman season, a teammate at Arizona, Orlando Vargas, asked me and Chris for a favor. He said that he had a gig to make a few extra bucks dancing at a bachelorette party in Tucson. Orlando asked us if we had ever been to a Mexican-style bachelorette party. We hadn't but he said the girls in Tucson could get pretty wild. He needed backup. It seemed like a fun deal, so Chris and I figured, why not?

It was a daytime party in someone's big backyard. Orlando had a cowboy outfit for the occasion. He asked us to put on two black tuxedos and wear sunglasses so we would look like professional security dudes. So we showed up and there were like twenty Latin chicks waiting on us.

As soon as we walked in, Orlando jumped right into his role and started dancing for the ladies, and they were happy. Orlando's dance moves were beyond funny. Chris and I somehow kept a straight face in our dark shades and tuxedos as Orlando busted out his cowboy dance moves.

It didn't take long for the women to start getting wild and feeding us margaritas. Before I knew it, they started recruiting me to take my clothes off and start dancing for them. I admit, they didn't have to put on the hard sell. I always wanted to dance for a big group of hot chicks and have them throw themselves at me, so I went for it. I stripped down to my white underwear, and the ladies liked it.

Chris was the responsible one and kept watch with his shades and tuxedo on while pounding tequila shots. Orlando was doing his thing and I kept trying to see what he was doing to learn some extra dance moves.

I don't know why, but I took it to the next level and got into the crowd looking for a girl to dance on. I took my white underwear and turned it into a man thong, which brought the craziness to an even higher level. They were aggressive.

There were a lot of hot, sexy Mexican ladies there but I picked out the largest, healthiest-looking one; she had to be 260 pounds, like I was. I wanted everyone at the party to be having fun, so I chose her. She was so happy I picked her. She went nuts. I was dancing and she was yelling all kinds of stuff at me and smacking my butt hard. Then I had her sit back in her chair and I got on top of her doing whatever dance moves I could think of.

Now, picture me at 260 pounds trying to dance to mariachi music. I was terrible at it. This wasn't my usual LMFAO-type music, but I didn't care. I was probably way off with my moves but they didn't care, either. They were on fire and the way they kept smacking my butt, I had a feeling I was going to be needing Chris's help to get out of there in one piece.

After ten seconds of me dancing on top of her in the chair, the collective 520 pounds of the two of us collapsed the folding chair. We crashed to the ground and I was on top. The crowd exploded with laughter. I got up and continued dancing (or twerking) to that mariachi music. That was the best thirty dollars I ever made!

11

THE BEGINNING

After the hazing and training camp were over, I couldn't wait to play in our first preseason game, at home against the Saints—the reigning Super Bowl champs. I played a lot in the game and did a ton of blocking on running and passing plays, but didn't get one ball thrown my way. They used me as a blocker and threw it to all the other tight ends and receivers. I was okay with that because I did a good job with my blocking. My tight ends coach, Brian Ferentz, was big on blocking and he was very happy with the way I did it. Throughout training camp I had been going up against Patriot defenders who were damn good, especially Rob Ninkovich. That sharpened my blocking skills and made me ready to block NFL defensive ends. I wasn't scared to block and get hurt.

I was scared to miss my block and get Tom Brady hurt. Those were some big guys flying around in the trenches, and they were tough to block, but I could do it. My number-one objective was to show everyone that I was the real deal in those trenches and I could block the big boys in this league. It was not about catching passes.

The problem with being a great blocking tight end is you can be looked at as one-dimensional, a better blocker than receiver. I knew I could catch the ball to make plays but I didn't say anything to the coaches about throwing me the ball. I was happy to get that first game under my belt, even if it was just preseason. I knew I would get my chance to catch the ball sooner or later and that when I got that chance, I would have to shine and take advantage of it. I was confident I could play. I didn't how good I would be but I was determined to find out.

The next preseason game was against Atlanta, on the road. It was second and ten at our 36-yard line. A pass play was called and I was supposed to stay in and block in case the outside linebacker blitzed. The defender dropped into coverage instead of coming in so I leaked out into the flat (toward the sideline) about one yard in front of the line of scrimmage as a reserve just in case no one was open. Tom came under pressure, and indeed no one was open, so he had to get rid of the ball and dumped it off to me, as I was hoping he would. When he lofted the short pass in the air, I was thinking, I'd better catch this. I stared that ball into my hands and body, and then when I had it, I thought, What do I do now? Well, right away two linebackers slammed into me and brought me down. It was a simple one-yard gain but it was awesome. I caught my first

I started early.
Partying on the beach
at four years old!

Gronkowski Christmas
family photo in 1994.
Left to right, top row:
Dan, Gord; bottom
row: Chris, Glenn,
and me.

Dressing crazy for the
party always came
naturally to me.

Chris, Gord, Gordy Sr., me, and Dan at Gord's Little League baseball event in 1993.

At the hospital on March 25, 1993, on the day Glenn was born. There I am, with a black eye, holding Glenn and sitting next to Chris, Gord, and Dan.

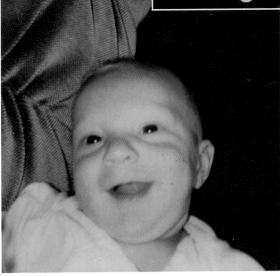

I've had the same goofy smile since 1989.

My eighth-grade JV
baseball shot, 2003.

Standing in front of our massive
collection of family trophies. Left
to right are Chris, Dan, Glenn,
me, and Gord.

Even as a kid I was a flirt.
Happily standing between two
cheerleaders in 1997.

Bobby Goon, John Ticco, Mojo Rawle me, and Papa Gron at a Miami Beach pool party, 2014.

Right before getting my first back surgery in college in 2009 at Dr. Watkins's facility.

On the squat rack, doing a photo shoot for Iovate in 2015.

What Glenn, Gord, Chris, Dan, and I were doing instead of getting suited up for the 2010 NFL Draft.

In disguise for Christmas shopping in 2011.

Spiking a puck during the Bruins game, February 2015.
(*ASSOCIATED PRESS Photo/Winslow Townson*)

Brady and I with the Vince Lombardi Trophy, celebrating our Super Bowl win. *(ASSOCIATED PRESS Photo/Michael Conroy)*

At the *Jimmy Kimmel Live* studio, right before shooting my segment. *(Cathy Gibson/Splash News/Corbis)*

Reacting to President Obama giving me a shout-out at the White House after the Super Bowl XLIX win. *(JONATHAN ERNST/ Reuters/Corbis)*

The Patriots Parade in Boston to celebrate our Super Bowl XLIX victory was . . . wild. Here I am, hanging out of a bus. *(ASSOCIATED PRESS photo/Charles Krupa)*

Patriots owner Robert Kraft and I after the emotional win against the Seahawks in Super Bowl XLIX. *(ROY DABNER/epa/Corbis)*

Flexing on the red carpet at the 2012 ESPY Awards. From left to right: Papa Gronk, Dan, Gord, me, and Chris. *(Byron Purvis/AdMedia/Corbis)*

Backstage at the ESPN shoot in 2014!

Me with my family, waiting to be drafted on the first night of the April 2010 NFL draft. From left to right: Gord; Dan; Glenn; Chris; my dad, Gordy Sr.; me; my mom, Diane; and Jason Rosenhaus.

About to score a touchdown in the first half of Super Bowl XLIX. *(Chris Coduto/Icon Sportswire/ Corbis)*

game pass from Tom Brady! Yes! Tom Brady! Damn it was fast, though. Those guys were on me superquick. This was a whole new level of speed to get adjusted to and because I wasn't confident with knowing my plays and had to think so much, I was not operating at a fast level.

Later in the game, Brian Hoyer was in at quarterback and he threw a touchdown pass to me. That was easy. I had caught a million passes from Brian since I worked with him the most in the off-season and in training camp, so we had really good chemistry. I wasn't good enough yet to be first string, so I got a ton of reps with Brian.

The touchdown was a third-and-six play at the Atlanta 24-yard line. When the play was called, I was fired up because I was really comfortable with Brian. I knew he would throw it to me if I got open. We ran it a lot in practice and I liked the route. At the snap, I faked the linebacker out, went right up the hash mark, and ran toward the end zone. Hoyer put it on the money, I jumped up, caught it, and ran in for the touchdown, just like we did in practice. That was my chance to show the team that I could make the play, and I did.

That second game was a solid step forward. I blocked well, ran routes well, and scored a touchdown. I made my share of rookie mistakes and got my share of criticism for it, though. I still needed to show Tom Brady what I could do.

Tom gave me my chance in the next game, against the St. Louis Rams, with two minutes left in the second quarter. We had the ball at the fourteen-yard line. When I looked at the defense, I knew the play would come to me. I put my hand in the dirt, took off when Tom hiked it, and ran a quick hook route, where I run straight about four yards and then hook right, taking a step toward the sideline. Tom was blitzed and threw it to me right away. I made up my mind that I was going to score no matter what and would show everyone that I was more than just a blocking tight end. I caught it at the ten-yard line and then got hit by linebacker James Laurinaitis at the seven-yard line. I wasn't going down and bounced off the hit, but he grabbed my leg at the six-yard line. I couldn't break free of his grip so I dragged him to the three-yard line and then dove, extending my arm and the ball just across the goal line before my knee touched down. The crowd and my teammates went wild. The play was reviewed and the touchdown stood. Everybody got fired up. Some in the media look back at that play and say it was the birth of Gronk.

Whether it was or wasn't, that play helped me out big-time. Tom decides who to throw to. I wanted to show him that I could make plays. I wanted him to see that if he threw it to me, he wouldn't regret it. But one play wasn't going to earn that kind of respect. I needed to show consistency; that's what the Patriots look for. I didn't want to be a one-time wonder. So when Tom threw me another ball at the start of the fourth quarter, I was going to make that catch, too, for another touchdown. The play was a twenty-yard route right up the middle between the safeties. Tom threw it up in the air and I went up and got it. I took the hit and pulled it down. When I went to the sideline, Pro Bowl running back Fred Taylor made a point of grabbing me and said, "You're going to be a Pro Bowl tight end one day, keep working hard." Coming from a great player like Fred, it meant a lot. I was starting to really believe in myself and making my teammates believers in me, too.

The next week, the final preseason game, I was treated like a starter and played only a few series like the rest of the starters. I felt great, though, and scored another touchdown from Tom in the first quarter. I was gaining confidence. I wasn't thinking about my back or about not getting hurt. I was just thinking to work hard, stay humble, know my playbook, and make the play when Tom threw it to me.

Training camp and the preseason were over. I wasn't tired or exhausted. I was fired up to prove myself to Tom, to my teammates, and coaches. My mind-set was to get the job done and show no weakness. I was ready for the season opener at home against the Bengals.

Scoring touchdowns in preseason with Tom was a definite confidence builder, but I was in a huddle with guys like Hall of Fame–caliber receiver Randy Moss, perennial Pro Bowl receiver Wes Welker, and Deion Branch, who all had a lot of great history with Tom. With those three receivers, I knew I wasn't going to get a lot of targets as a rookie. I was just very happy to be playing in our opener and doing whatever Coach Belichick asked of me to help us win. My goal for the season was to get the playbook down, improve on my blocking, and learn how to run NFL-caliber routes. I wasn't thinking that Tom needed to throw me the ball. I was thinking

I needed to do whatever Tom needed me to do. If that meant blocking on passing downs instead of catching passes, I was fine with that. I was a rookie and needed to pay my dues and earn respect.

With the Bengals, I pretty much blocked the whole game, like I did in the first preseason game. They didn't get any sacks on Tom and I was very proud of my pass blocking to keep him on his feet instead of on his back. I got only one target pass thrown my way and it was for only one yard, but this was a big one.

It was third and goal at the Cincinnati one-yard line. Tom called the play and I knew if I got off the line fast and could run past the linebacker to get open toward the corner of the end zone, he would throw it to me. We had practiced it a lot and I knew I had to make a play. I wanted to make the big catch and deliver for Tom, because when he throws it to you and it's a big play, if you catch it, he will throw it to you again. If you don't make the play, he will throw it to someone else who *will* make the play, and that's how it should be.

When we broke the huddle, I lined up on the right side of the offensive line and put my hand in the dirt. As soon as it was snapped, I shot in between the defenders and raced past the linebacker toward the corner of the end zone. Tom threw it up high where only I could jump up to get it and I scored my first NFL touchdown with my first NFL catch! Yes! Hell yeah! I was screaming at the top of my lungs.

That score put the game out of reach in the fourth quarter. I didn't think too much, just focused on catching the ball like we had done in practice many times. Because I ran so hard and jumped just right and caught the ball where I should have from a technique standpoint, it was easy. My teammates chest-bumped me and Tom came over to give me a fist pump. I still have no idea why, but I handed him the ball. I didn't really know what I was doing. I was just happy and relieved that I had come through for my team. I did get to save the ball.

The next day, I was really fired up to get into the meeting room to watch the film of the game. I wasn't looking for a pat on the back. I was just happy not to be the poster boy for screwing up. I thought I would get some praise but it didn't happen that way in the meetings. I was still a rookie, it had been my first game, and Tom was very tough on me. Whatever I did wrong, Tom let me know that I had to do it right.

There was no time for any praise, only time to get ready to play the New York Jets on the road. It was pretty much the same role for me to be primarily a blocking tight end. I had one catch for fourteen yards and that was it. I would have been okay with it if we had won the game, but we lost 28–14 and it felt like the end of the world in the locker room after the game. I wasn't happy with my game—my blocking wasn't great, and I was still learning the ropes. I didn't make any big mental mistakes but I wasn't getting open on my routes. I wasn't familiar with the defensive coverages. Getting open was hard for me.

Next up was my hometown team, the Bills, and I was super-pumped. It was a very close game into the late third quarter, with the score 24–23 in our favor. On third and five at the Bills' five-yard line, I got open in the end zone. Tom saw me and threw it to me for the touchdown. This time, instead of handing him the ball, I spiked it. That was my very first Gronk spike!

I didn't know that would be my trademark touchdown celebration; it just happened that way. Tom was gaining confidence in me as a red-zone, end-zone guy to throw to. We went on to win the game and I helped the team get the W with my touchdown. It didn't matter that I had only three targets. This was a big game for me, because while I was still viewed as the blocking tight end, I was now viewed as a 6′6″, long-armed, fast weapon in the red zone (inside the opponent's twenty-yard line) for scoring touchdowns. Tom and I were building chemistry in the end zone. After the game, I was really fired up because I had blown up some linebackers in the blocking game, scored a TD, and beat my hometown team. It was a big game for me.

Next up was *Monday Night Football* against the Dolphins, at Miami. I couldn't wait to play my first Monday night game on national TV. The beginning of the game had fireworks; it was a crazy atmosphere and I was amped up. Again in the game I mostly blocked, and had one target for one catch, four yards. We got the win, and I contributed as a blocker to protect Tom and to aid the running game. I wanted to do more. I wanted to catch the ball and show everyone that I was a complete tight end, but I didn't have a great week of practice, but until you prove it in practice, you don't get your chance in the game. I was still learning the offense, still making Tom mad with my little mistakes, and I needed to be more consistent.

Next up we were home against the Ravens. Different game,

same story. One target, one catch for twenty-four yards, but we won. I blocked well and was earning respect as a tough blocker in the trenches with the big boys. Again we won, so I was happy. I wanted to do more as a receiver and kept working at it in practice to show I could be trusted in that role.

We hit the road for San Diego to take on the Chargers. More of the same. I was scrapping in the trenches, had two targets for two catches totaling ten yards. Tom threw 32 passes and only two went to me, but one was for a one-yard touchdown in the first quarter. We won again, I blocked well, caught the two passes thrown my way, scored a touchdown, and did my part. I didn't let myself get upset about not getting more targets. I was a rookie, I had to pay my dues. I was still learning, and we were winning, which was the bottom line.

After a home game against the Vikings in which I blocked well and played well but had only one catch for five yards, it was time for a road game at the 2-5 Cleveland Browns. Their head coach, Eric Mangini, used to coach for Coach Belichick, and the media claimed there was bad blood arising out of the whole "spygate" controversy, which caused a lot of trouble and aggravation for our team. I didn't know much about it and didn't care. We were focused on getting the win. I had a good week of practice so this was the game where I was finally going to get more passes thrown my way.

I got my wish with eight passes thrown my way but it turned into a nightmare. On the first drive of the game, the Browns moved the ball and scored a field goal to go up 3–0. On the kickoff right afterward, the ball was short and came toward me. I should have called for a fair catch but I thought I heard my teammate wave me off to leave it for him. At the last minute, I did the worst thing— nothing. I didn't fair-catch it, I didn't block the defender coming for the ball, and as a result, the Browns recovered the ball at our 21-yard line. Just two plays later they scored a touchdown to go up 10–0.

That was the first huge mistake I made with the Patriots and it really hurt us. We scored to make it 10–7 and then they scored to make it 17–7.

Toward the end of the second quarter, we had momentum and drove the ball down to their nine-yard line. On first and goal, Tom threw me a short pass and I wanted to drag everyone into the end zone with me. While I was fighting to get to the goal line, I wasn't careful with the ball and fumbled it away. So instead of scoring and us being down only three points at the half, I turned it over and we went into halftime down 17–7. I was trying to make amends for my bad play earlier and ended up making things twice as worse.

We never recovered from that play and were defeated, 34–14. I felt like I had lost the game for us. If I had handled the kickoff properly and had not fumbled the ball, we likely would have won. Yes, they ran the ball down our throats, with Peyton Hillis running 29 times for 184 yards and two touchdowns, but this is a game of momentum and turnovers change it.

Although we were doing well overall at 7-2, it seemed more like we were 2-7. I did not look forward to sitting in the meeting room on Monday. After my botched kickoff and fumble, I was a sitting duck. Given that Tom could be tough on me even after a win or a good personal performance, I was expecting to get really whacked now, but it didn't happen. No one pointed fingers and instead we had a very intense week of practice.

What Tom and my coaches noticed was that other than those two terrible mistakes, I had made four excellent plays and had my best blocking game yet. So instead of that game hurting my confidence, it actually helped it. I put the negative stuff out of my mind and worked extra hard in practice to get better and get ready for the Steelers at Pittsburgh.

I have to say that receiver Wes Welker helped me out a lot that year. He was a hard worker, a perfectionist down to the smallest detail. I tried to learn as much as I could from him. His routes were amazing and his ability to find the open spot in coverage was brilliant. Most of all, he took the time to work with me on all the little things I needed to do better in order to get good at selling routes and running routes the way Tom liked them run. Even though I was eight inches taller, I really looked up to Wes. He helped me get ready for game time.

The very first pass Tom threw in the next game was toward me. I wasn't worried that if I dropped it Tom would stop throwing the ball to me. I was just hungry to win my battle. So when it came my way, I caught that pass for 7 yards. Two plays later I caught another one for 12 yards. Five plays later, the play was called for me to race up the middle 19 yards toward the goal line. I had a fast defensive back covering me. As soon as the ball was snapped, I ran as fast as I could to get a slight step on him. I barely had separation, but

I had the advantage of reach. Tom fired that ball in the only possible place I could reach it. The ball soared just beyond the defender's reach and I grabbed it a split second before the safety came down to hit me. It was an insane throw and I made the big catch!

I was now three catches for three targets and a beautiful TD on our opening drive. I was making amends for last week and hungry for more. My next two passes were completions but both times there was a penalty to nullify the play. At the start of the third quarter, Tom threw me the ball in the end zone for a nine-yard score. Midway in the fourth quarter, Tom threw it to me again for a 25-yard touchdown where I was able to run full speed and get separation from the defensive back. I pulled off a hat trick and it was awesome!

We won! I went 5 for 5 with 72 yards and 3 touchdowns. It felt great coming off the worst game of my career to then have by far my best game. We were back on track with the win and I was back on track to scoring more touchdowns. The sting of last week's loss was gone. What mattered most to me was that coming off a losing game where I had messed up big-time, Tom, Coach O'Brien, and Coach Belichick didn't beat me up and turn away. Instead they came right back with some tough love and gave me the chance to redeem myself and make things right. They could have put me on the shelf and kept me as a blocker but instead they gave me the chance to be a complete tight end weapon in all phases of the game.

I felt like when I went up against the linebacker, I was too fast for him to cover me. When I went up against a cornerback or safety, I was too big for him to stop me from catching the ball.

I believed I was a mismatch in coverage no matter who they put in front of me.

I wanted to show consistency and have another monster game but the next week, home against the Colts, I had one ball thrown my way. It was a nice 25-yard play, where I caught the ball down the middle, bounced off the safety, and it took three other guys to tackle me. The rest of the game I did a ton of blocking. We won against a tough Peyton Manning team so I was happy, but it felt like a step back with only one catch. I wasn't mad at Tom or the coaches. I was mad at myself. I thought whatever passes I got were earned. If I didn't get more, it was because I didn't earn them. When I had a consistent week of doing everything right in practice, I got the ball thrown my way. When I was inconsistent, I didn't get the ball as much. It was a merit system and I was fine with that.

It reminded me a bit of my college days, where I was on a roller-coaster ride, but this time we were winning. We went to Detroit next and beat them 45–24. Tom threw five passes to me and I made the play on all five throws. No touchdowns, but we won and I was happy being 9-2.

Up next was the Jets, who had beat us on the road in the second game of the season. This time, we were the home team and we were looking for payback on *Monday Night Football*. And we got it, crushing them 45–3. It was awesome but once again a quiet night for me on *Monday Night Football*. I had one catch for 12 yards and no TDs but we won and were now 10-2. And I blocked really well, so I was cool.

Coming off that big Monday night win, I thought the meetings and practices would be a little easier on me. I was dead wrong. We worked on one route in practice where I was supposed to run about ten yards to the end zone and then turn around. I didn't run it exactly the way Tom wanted me to and he got so mad at me I thought he was going to throw a punch. He tore into me and I wanted to get in his face, but he was Tom Brady—the guy was the best in the league and I was a rookie. I had to just take my beating like a man, but I was at my limit. There was nothing I could do but prove myself, so I worked on that stop route over and over again until I got it perfectly right.

The stop route is designed for me to run right up the middle, stop to get separation from the linebacker just as I get into the end zone, and then immediately turn around. You can't stop too early or too late. The idea is for the linebacker to be in contact with you as you both race down the field and at the goal line use your shoulder to get physical and bounce off him, separate, and turn around. You have to get physical at the right time and separate. You have to box him out with your shoulder. You also have to sell the linebacker that you are going to the back of the end zone so he keeps running at full momentum with you. When Tom sees me have that contact, he is supposed to immediately fire the ball in there so when I turn around, it goes right into my chest. Timing is everything and I struggled with it in practice. Eventually I got the hang of it but that practice was not pretty and I thought Tom had had it with me.

So when Tom called that play in the first quarter against the Bears, I got dead serious and fired up. The weather in Chicago at Soldier Field was brutal. The field was white with snow, it was freezing out, and I was going up against All-Pro linebacker Brian Urlacher, who was one of the best cover linebackers in the league. Not too many tight ends put their shoulder into Brian Urlacher's chest on routes and get physical with him, but that was exactly what I was going to do. This was my big chance to earn respect in this league and I wanted it.

When we broke the huddle and snapped the ball at the seven-yard line, I ran right toward Urlacher. I gave him a stutter-step, shoulder-fake move and hit his chest with my shoulder. The impact pushed him upright and to the left. I stopped and turned around to the right. Tom threw it exactly as I hit Urlacher. He threw it low and outside—precisely where it had to be. I caught it with my hands and body to make sure I tucked it in and scored. It was the perfect throw and the perfect route. I made the play just like I was supposed to do it in practice. I did it right and from that play on, Tom never treated me like a rookie again. He went from being supercritical to supercool.

That was when I realized why Tom was so hard on me. Tom didn't want me to be good, he wanted me to be great. He was so demanding and pushed me to my limit because he wanted me to be the best. Tom saw my potential and knew that if I worked the way he and Wes worked, I could be a Pro Bowl player. He wanted me to be a smart perfectionist at my craft, like he was. He didn't want me to do things any other way but at my best. No rookie could have had a better mentor than Tom. I really appreciate that now, but I admit I didn't during those first thirteen games. I went from not understanding why he was so hard on me to understanding that the whole time he was being great to me. It's kind of like a drill sergeant who you think wants to make your life miserable throughout boot camp but once you make it through, you always are grateful to him for helping you.

We beat the bears 36–7. We went on to beat the Packers at home and although I had only one catch for 25 yards, I realized that in the NFL, not every week is going to be a huge one. The offensive game plan is different every week and you have to adjust to the opposing defense. We were now 12-2 and I was happy to be part of a winning team.

The next game was extra special for me because it was at Buffalo, in front of my hometown crowd. For the first time, Tom threw more passes to me than any of the other receivers. We were gelling. I scored two touchdowns and led the team in receiving with 4 catches for 54 yards in a dominating win over the Bills, 34–3.

We were now 13-2 with the final game at home versus the Miami Dolphins. Once again Tom targeted me more than anyone else and I led the team in receiving with 6 catches for 102 yards, including a 28-yard touchdown. We won 38–7 and finished the regular season with a 14-2 record. I closed that season out playing in all sixteen games, catching 42 passes for 546 yards and 10 touchdowns. That was something to be proud of, but now it was time for the playoffs.

Our first playoff game would be on our turf, at Gillette Stadium against the Jets. We were undefeated at home that season and hadn't lost anywhere in a while. We were hot and were ready. At least I thought we were. The Jets' head coach, Rex Ryan, had a great defensive game plan and our offense struggled to make plays. In what was a painful upset, the Jets beat us 28–21. This was the same Jets team we had beat earlier in the season at home, 45–3. They just played better and beat us.

I thought we were headed for the Super Bowl and instead we lost and it was all over. Everything we worked to accomplish as a team was taken from us and all the wins that year meant nothing. I learned how tough it is to end the season with a loss. I had a solid game with four catches for a team-leading 65 yards but I had no touchdowns and we didn't get the job done.

It left a bitter taste in my mouth. I had been through adversity before and I knew we would work hard to come back next year. At the same time, I appreciated that I went through a tough rookie learning process and finished strong. I improved leaps and bounds from my first days at training camp. I knew that with a good off-season, I would come back recharged and better than before. I also knew that it was time to have some fun!

12

PARTY ROCKERS!

I was proud of what I accomplished my 2010 rookie year. I put up good numbers, blocked well overall, and set some rookie records. Against the Steelers, I became the first Patriot rookie and the youngest NFL rookie to score the hat trick—three TDs. I was the first rookie tight end in over forty years to score ten touchdowns. Most important, I made every practice and played in every game.

It was a long grind from the moment I was drafted in April until the season ended in January 2011. I had been on a nonstop mission to get into shape and get ready to play football since I injured my back in the summer of 2009. It was a marathon, starting with the brutal ordeal of my back injury, then the surgery, then the physical therapy, then the training to get back to form, then getting ready for training camp, and then playing twenty-one games from preseason to the playoffs. Along the way, I lost my junior year of football and fun. When I declared by January 15 for the 2010 NFL Draft, I gave up my senior year of college. Now I hadn't partied at all and had basically been in a meat grinder for a year and a half straight. I needed a break, I needed to recharge, I needed to party!

For the first time, I had the money to enjoy myself and treat my family and friends to some fun. My friends from high school and college were seniors and so I took some flights to visit with them. I traveled all around the country and always managed to get a workout in wherever I went. But I also knew I had a lot of partying to do to make up for lost time. And nobody, and I mean nobody, parties like my crew, the Party Rockers.

Wherever we go, whatever we do, when the boys are all together, we rock the house and take it to the craziest level. We like alcohol and occasionally overdo it, but we don't need it to have a good time. We don't do drugs—that's for people who don't know how to party straight. We don't hurt people or look for any trouble. All we do is get wild, dance like madmen, and have a very fun time.

At my brother Dan's weekend bachelor party in Vegas, we broke all the records. It's hard to remember a lot of what happened and I talked to the crew to piece together that weekend in June 2011 so I could re-create the monumental, epic partying that took place.

It started on a hot Friday afternoon when the cast of characters arrived. There must have been thirty guys there, some I was meeting for the first time who were friends of Dan or Gord. Dan's college football teammate at Maryland, who is now known as professional wrestler Mojo Rawley to WWE fans across the country, set the tempo by sending out bios on the cast of characters so the newcomers to the group would know what to expect.

Here's the bio Mojo sent out to the guys on my oldest brother, Gord:

A.K.A. "The Captain." As the oldest Gronk brother, this former professional baseball star and current professional big brother calls the shots, he makes the moves, and ensures that everyone's always as positive as possible. He is an optimist and writes the blueprints for our party rocking trips by picking the cities, and getting us set up at whatever club or party we want to attend. He is the glue that holds the team together and when he is missing, things just aren't the same. Gordie is a team player, he keeps everyone's self confidence as high as the sky, even while all the girls are scratching and clawing at his silky smooth body! And for some reason they always do because he constantly looks like he got mauled by a cougar: both the animal and type of woman! His resiliency is amazing, as he seems to somehow rally through injury, drinks, and unfavorable conditions to stay turned up all the time!

The bio on the next-oldest brother, Dan:

A.K.A. "The Brains." Dan looks like he is straight out of the movie 300 except he doesn't need the CGI! He is tall, he is chiseled, and all the chix unanimously agree that he is very handsome. Dan is also the responsible one, and is the only one on the team that is no longer a bachelor. Even though we all are not thrilled to lose our brother to the institution of marriage, Dan's bride-to-be is a cool chick, rages hard, and brings all her girlfriends around, so it's OK by us! Constantly looking out for his teammates and preventing us from engaging in problematic scenarios, Dan uses his brains and great looks to lure chix into the party rock lair and then pass them along to us. Therefore he is the official chix recruiter and wingman for the team. Dan displays his dedication to the team by always providing valuable assists, which is why he has locked down the team's unsung hero award!!!

The bio on Chris:

A.K.A. "The One Seed." Chris is a genius and could have gone to Harvard to play football but told them no thanks, for the sole reason that they don't party. Chris is a wild man. Whether he's throwing spine-crushing and punishing blocks or dominating every party he's ever been to, Chris has an affinity for nudity and he gets so wild that we lose him a lot. He frequently disappears off the grid. But we never worry. Chris is a survivor and we usually find him facedown somewhere, or in a DJ booth after he abducted it. Chris is reminiscent of the legendary Vince Lombardi: he will leave it all on the field partying until he collapses, even if he collapses in the middle of the street, a dance floor, or on the floor of the library, because it's all happened before.

The bio on Glenn "Goose":

A.K.A. "The Wrecking Ball." Goose is the definition of reckless abandon. He is the youngest member but perhaps the most insane. Living up to the legacy that was laid down by his brothers, Goose studied the ways of the Party Gronk closely throughout his youth and adolescence. This kind of observation and attention to detail is perhaps why Goose is one of the top up-and-coming student athletes in the country. Insanity and brilliance may sound like an oxymoron to some, but it is all part of his master plan. Some say the Party Rockers cannot change the world, but Glenn is our hope for the next generation.

The bio on Gordy Sr.:

A.K.A. "The Innovator." Big G has taken party rocking to epic proportions over the past decades. A former college and pro football star himself, he has redefined party rocking year after year and he has established the precedent for us to live by. Big G will go down in history as one of the most legendary fathers in the history of the world. Cultivating four professional athletes with one more to come, fathers all over the world yearn to be like Big G. Perhaps that is why countless people have offered Big G big money to purchase his sperm so they can have the children of champions themselves. It's not every day you can see a father hang with his sons on the dance floor, and it's even more rare to have a father whose sons constantly get rejected by chix because they would rather hit on their dad instead. Women of all ages fall head over heels for the jackedness and dieselness of Big G, and his dance moves . . . Don't even get us started on his awesome dance moves! He is a successful entrepreneur, a successful father, and the innovator of the Party Rockers!

Dan and Gordy did the bio on Mojo, who back then was known as Dean:

A.K.A. "The Hype Man!" Mojo doesn't get hyped, he stays hyped. This NFL defensive lineman brings levels of hype that this world has never seen to any location he is in. He has the never-before-seen ability to single-handedly transform any setting into a rage fest! Give Mojo literally 6.9 seconds in any quiet, relaxed, and conservative room where people are just sitting and chilling, and Mojo will have people on their feet dancing and jumping around like they never have before. And it doesn't matter if it is a club, an arena, a restaurant, or even a library. Mojo is the hype man, a party rock visionary rocking his Zubaz outfit head to toe that never sleeps nor staggers.

Before or during party rock events, Mojo delivers legendary pregame speeches that fire up his team so much they are ready to tear the world apart, just as he does on the football field. The Party Rockers never have to worry about finding chix if Mojo is around because they always flock to him, his dance moves, and his amazingly fast hips that put cheetahs to shame! He is undefeated in dance contests, and you can guarantee it with any money in the world that if Mojo is there, everyone will have the best time of their lives.

The bio on me:

A.K.A. "The Superstar!" Rob is rated the #1 party rocker in all of pro sports. He is the superstar, he is the main attraction, the headliner, and there has never been a player in history in any sport that exemplifies excellence in the field of play in addition to the field of party rock. Men want to be him and chix want to be with him. His humility is astounding, which combined with his body builder physique, leaves women utterly susceptible to his charm! The weekend just cannot possibly be as wild if the superstar isn't there. Rob has no filter, he doesn't change who he is for anybody, and he lives his life how he sees fit. Whereas other athletes might be exhausted and want to go ice down and go to sleep, Rob rises above pain and injuries to party rock at all times and is unfazed and unintimidated by any obstacle that may stand in his path.

Next up is Bobby Goon, a friend of ours:

> *A.K.A. "The Utility Man." He is the bodyguard, the driver, the confidant; he is the utility man. Bringing an iron fist of protection to the Party Rockers, Goon keeps all members out of legal and social trouble. With a sixth sense that would put both Bruce Willis and Spider-Man to shame, Goon can sniff out a potential issue well before it has even brewed and silence it with ruggedness. He ensures that no pictures or videos are ever taken, and can single-handedly protect us from an army of paparazzi, no problem. A man who enjoys fine foods, or any types of food at all, Goon also provides us with Drunk Goggles Security. Anytime one of us is going to make a mistake and take home a less than optimal chick, Goon steps in to the rescue to protect him . . . unless it's Gord . . . there's no protecting Gord. Whenever Goon is around we can all take a deep sigh of relief and let it all hang out because we know we are taken care of.*

So now you know the crew. When we read the bios and stepped off the plane in Vegas, we could feel the energy in the desert air. We couldn't wait for all the boys to get together and we were fired up to get after it. We started our Friday night with a dinner so that we could all get reacquainted and put the game plan into effect.

After that, everyone has a different recollection and story, but what first happened from there is we had our pregame speech ritual.

"Hype Man" Mojo Rawley, dressed in bright neon-looking Zubaz striped pants and tank top, gathered everyone around and got us crazy fired up with a pregame speech.

Picture a 6'3", 269-pound muscle dude who looks like a professional wrestler and now is dressed in neon-colored Zubaz pants with his back turned to us. Everyone is waiting on his speech with crazy anticipation. He takes his time, stares out the window at the Vegas skyline with dead-serious intensity and intimidation, and begins:

"One of the great questions of the world . . . is when will the bubble burst."

Wearing bright yellow sunglasses on his forehead, he turns around and faces us as if we are getting ready for battle. He looks at us with emotion in his eyes, and continues.

"We've traveled the world together, men . . ." Then he whispers "the whole world" as he walks toward us.

Looking ready to fight, he adds, "Every place we've gone . . . we've destroyed it! We've obliterated it! But with this kind of domination . . . there comes complacency!"

Looking angry, he starts to raise his voice: "Complacency that stems from . . . I'm tired of domination. Where is the challenge . . ."

Now in full yell, "I've done everything we can do! I've dominated every club! I've dominated every pool party! So what's my motivation?"

Looking enraged, he blasts us: "There's been a lot of disappointment I've seen today. I've partied with some of my best friends in the world that are embarrassed to wear Zubaz to clubs now. Dammit! That makes my blood boil!"

Then he turns to Gord and points with anger, saying, "This dude right here took about forty damn minutes to get ready for the club. And this is the problem I'm talkin' about. Complacency!!!"

Now yelling at the top of his lungs: "But tonight . . . the Party Rockers have reunited and they have descended upon the mean streets of Vegas. . . ."

Gord is so fired up he can't contain himself anymore and seconds him, yelling, "Ye-es!"

Mojo's on fire! He's yelling like a madman. "So we're gonna take complacency and shove it right where the sun don't shine! 'Cause this is not how we roll! We got a shot at redemption tonight! And we're gonna lay it all on the line. 'Cause this is what we do! This is what Party Rockers stand for! And I don't care how you feel!"

Mojo has everyone screaming and then he settles us down, quietly commanding us, "Because tonight we will party rock! Not because we want to . . ."

And now he's getting louder and louder, into a frenzy: "not because we need to, but because we must share our talents with the world! Because this is what we do!"

At the peak of his speech, he concludes with his trademark line, which we've all been waiting for: "We don't get hyped . . . we stay hyped!"

With goose bumps all over, adrenaline rushing, and chills running down our spines, we went nuts! We huddled up, jumped up and down, and were hooting, hollering, barking, and just getting out of control. In the middle of the mayhem, I yelled, "Let's go!"

We attacked Vegas without mercy. When we walked in the door at the first club of the night, the first thing on our mind wasn't picking up hot chicks. It was all about seeing who could get crazy and rock the place. We got kicked out of there within thirty minutes. While I was dancing on a stripper pole, Gord was dancing on the couches, taking his shirt off, getting crazy, so before we got into it with the bouncers, we left. As soon as Gord walked out of the club, I got a running head start and chop-blocked Gord from the side. He went down hard and had no idea what happened. He grabbed his knee in pain and my dad got pissed off. He thought our friend Jimmy Bieber did it.

Big G got scary and grabbed Jimmy, yelling in his face, "What did you do to my boy!" We had to hold my dad back and settle him down. From there we went to two more clubs. In one of them, Mojo was dancing with his shirt off and swinging it around over his head. He's usually super-sweaty and when he was swinging the shirt, sure enough sweat was flying everywhere. It kind of created a circle around him and spread out the dance floor like rotor wash from a helicopter. Mojo's shirt accidentally got caught on a small chandelier and knocked some glass out of it. The glass all rained down on Chris's head. The little pieces of glass stuck to him like glue. Standing there, his blond hair turned red with blood, Chris just said, "Wow, that sucks!" and continued partying.

I looked like I had just seen a ghost. My dad had been having as much fun as anyone until that happened, since he's so used to his boys being crazy and stupid, but now he just said, "Well, that's not good." The owner of the bar came racing over and said to Mojo, "Did you even see what you just did?" My dad calmed the guy down and smoothed it over. Chris, Mojo, Gord, and I got crazy all over again and the crowd got so out of hand that the owner loved it and didn't make us pay for anything. That is a typical outcome and lets us get away with taking our shirts off and causing a decent amount of damage here and there.

We got two or three hours of sleep before our standards demanded that we wake each other up and keep party rocking around the clock. We went to a big pool party Saturday afternoon. The head bouncer came up to us and said he heard we had got kicked out of the club the night before for getting crazy and we should know he would kick us out if we got too insane there, too. We said no problem and then got crazy anyway. Chicks were throwing their tops and everyone was having so much fun the bouncer couldn't kick us out.

Pool parties are our favorite. There is always plenty of room to dance crazy, a lot of loud music, hot babes in bikinis, plenty of drinks in the hot sun; it's a blast. When the girls see us dancing, they try to keep up and hang with us, but they can't. We dance so fast, so hard, they can't resist the challenge of partying like we do. Nothing gets girls more ready to party than dancing.

Chris got so hammered that when it came time to go to the club, he jumped into a taxi and told the guy to take him there. The driver said, "Sir, you are here. It is right through the door there." He had just walked right past it. The driver told him again.

Chris wasn't hearing it and insisted that the guy drive and take him there. Eventually Chris threw him a hundred-dollar bill and told him to just get him there. So the driver drove off, circled around for a minute, and then said, "Okay, we're here." Chris thanked him, got out, and walked into the same hotel he had just walked out of.

After spending a couple hours at the pool, me, Gord, Mojo, and our friend Dana Parenteau got these four dimes (hot chicks rated a 10) to come up to our room. We had an awesome two-story suite with a huge couch and a good-looking spread of food on the table. We were all hungry and let the girls go first. There was cheese, fruits, olives, nuts, and a bag of potato chips. The hottest one said, "Mmmm," as she excitedly grabbed the chip bag.

Well, we didn't know it at the time, but one of the other members of the crew had left a surprise in the bag for us. Evidently someone couldn't find the toilet and took a dump in it.

As she unrolled the bag and opened it, the smell took over the room. She looked up at us and we already knew what had happened. I'll never forget the grossed-out, angry look on her face when she asked, "Is that poop?"

It was so funny, we just exploded with laughter. We laughed so hard, we didn't even care that the girls walked out. We just couldn't believe someone got us like that. The bottom line was that we had to avenge ourselves. It wasn't hard to track down who the culprit was and he came clean. I'm not going to throw him under the bus, but rest assured we got even with him.

Several hours later, he was with us in our suite when we and a new group of girls ordered a bunch of burgers from room service to refuel. When he went to the bathroom, one of us who I won't identify took a burger, pulled out the beef patty, and got intimate with the patty and his frank and beans, if you know what I mean. We put the burger back and grabbed all the burgers except for that one and another. When he came out of the bathroom, we were all eating our burgers except for Gord. Gord said to him, "Hey, grab a burger, these are awesome!"

Gord grabbed the other one (the clean one) and left the one that had the frank-and-beans treatment. As soon as he took a bite, the girls were laughing, and as he started chowing down on the burger, we began chanting, "Burger boy! Burger boy!" Eventually we told him, but not until after he had finished eating it.

Next up was a bit of beer pong in which Gord lost and Chris won. The punishment for losing? The loser had to lie still on a table while the winner jumped high into the air from another table and landed an atomic elbow right into the loser's body. It was a tough weekend for Gord. The night before he got his knee whacked by my chop block and that night, in a supercrowded room with fifty people cheering him on, he took a brutal flying elbow from Chris that sent them smashing through the wood table. Gord took it like a man. At least, he didn't feel any pain until he got home and the alcohol wore off.

We hit the club scene. Mojo the wild man climbed fifteen feet above the dance floor to reach a small platform. The first thing we look for anytime we walk into a club is a stage to dance on or a net or wire we can swing from. Mojo found his spot and was dancing like a maniac. It was such a small platform, I was sure he was going to fall off. But then a hot chick waved him down to come dance.

So I climbed up to the platform and started dancing even crazier than Mojo had. I wanted to one-up Mojo so I was jumping up and down on the platform. The only problem was that Mojo had sweated like a pig all over the platform and it was superslippery. Well, you can probably figure out what happened from there. My back foot slipped off the platform and I fell straight down next to where Mojo was dancing with these two hot girls. I landed right on one of them and knocked her through a glass table. She totally broke my fall. The glass shattered and exploded. I was in a daze and was thinking my dad was going to beat the hell out of me for this.

The whole place went silent. Mojo and I were scared to touch her and pull her out of the glass, because we didn't want to make things worse. I was scared she was dead. Mojo and I looked at each other and were like, "Oh sh-t!" Thank God she started moving. We helped her to her feet. But she was bleeding and all messed up. Everyone was still silent and in shock. Then she threw her hair back and yelled, "Give me another shot!"

The entire place cheered her on. Her girlfriends took her to the bathroom, cleaned her up, and then came back and partied! She said to us, "You're not the only hyped ones who can party!" I was so impressed I took her as my date to Dan's wedding. Chicks love partying with the Party Rockers, so much that they are willing to endure a 6′6″, 260-pound man falling fifteen feet through the air and landing directly on top of them, resulting in their head crashing through a glass table. They are willing to go through all of that just to party with us.

The next morning our suite was totally annihilated. There was a fifteen-foot spider crack in the middle of the green marble floor and no one could figure out how that could happen to such a hard surface. The huge square couch that we used as a wrestling ring had blood, alcohol, and chocolate all over it. The TVs were shattered. There was a TV in the hot tub, fortunately not plugged in. There were teeth sitting on the counter and we still don't know whose they were.

Sweet Pete went home with a black eye and our friend Mike Leuhrson went home with a broken hand. He tried turning the suite into a slip-and-slide. While doing some break-dancing move spinning on his hand, he broke it. Despite all this adversity, we made it back in time for Dan's wedding, which was awesome. At the wedding party, each table had a three-foot-high glass vase with flowers. Chris took one of them, threw out the flowers, and filled it with beer. He walked around and had everybody chug it.

It was a crazy off-season and exactly what I needed to recharge my batteries.

Everyone has pressure and problems and I deal with mine by working hard to make things better. At the same time, having fun helps keep the pressure off and it doesn't hurt to let loose and not care what other people think. Don't let other people stop you from having fun. I stand for working hard to be your best and partying hard to enjoy yourself along the way. Look at my dad: here's a guy in his fifties who stays in great shape, has five great kids, works hard at his business, and can still have as much fun as anyone half his age. If he isn't winning, I don't know who is. I want to see you win too and it starts by being happy and having fun.

That's what I did in the summer of 2011, and it got me ready. It was now time to play some more football for the New England Patriots.

13

THE SUPER BOWL

Yes, I definitely had fun that 2011 off-season. Meanwhile, I couldn't do any work at the team facility with the Patriots because there was an NFL lockout, which prevented me from getting inside the building. All team activities were shut down. We didn't have any off-season workouts, practices, or camps at all until the lockout ended in late July. But I made sure to get my workouts in elsewhere.

Orlando Vargas, my former teammate at Arizona, is a beast of a workout warrior and I spent a lot of time in Arizona training with him. Working out with Orlando, Chris, and Dan that off-season had me in the best shape of my life. Instead of working to get my legs back or my speed and agility back, I was feeling 100 percent after the season and was now working to get bigger, faster, and stronger than I had ever been before. It was a monster difference between working to get ahead and working to come back.

It was also night and day between this August and the last one, in 2010. That year in training camp, I had been overwhelmed. I was trying to get the playbook down, and I was trying to get used to the speed, power, shiftiness, and technique of the defensive ends I had to block. I was learning how to read defensive coverages to find the open area. I was learning how to run routes in the precise way that Tom wants his tight ends to run them. I was trying to earn Tom's trust to be his go-to guy. I was trying to get used to the speed of the defensive players covering me. I was trying to get used to traveling over the long haul of the preseason, a sixteen-game regular season, and then the postseason. I was trying to understand how to prepare myself physically and mentally to play each game and above all this I was trying to learn the ropes of being an NFL player with the New England Patriots—the most disciplined and the best-coached team in the NFL. All of those challenges took a lot of time, but I felt confident that I now knew what I was doing. Except perhaps for one thing. I wasn't sure I had earned Tom's trust to look to me when he needed the big play.

Coming off a healthy rookie season and off-season of great workouts, I was confident in myself. Now, I pride myself on being a humble guy and I never would have said this publicly, but I told my close friend John Ticco, whom I grew up with as a kid, that I was going to have the best year any tight end ever had and break every NFL tight end record there is. To the media, I always do my best to show humility because I believe in being humble with what you say and in how you treat people. I'm the same guy in private, but I do tell my close friends and families what I want to accomplish. I was trained to be the best tight end ever since I was a boy. I felt ready to work for it and do it. To be the hands-down best ever, you have to win a Super Bowl. That's the ultimate goal and I figured if I had my best season, we could indeed win it all.

Day one of making that happen started with training camp. As I said, the lockout ended in July, and since I trained so hard with Orlando, Chris, and Dan, I was off to a fantastic start. My blocking was at an all-time high, I felt superstrong, I had my technique down, and I was quick enough to handle anyone. On passing plays, I was constantly getting open and catching everything thrown my way. I couldn't wait for the first preseason game because I wanted to let the league know that this was going to be my year. I really believed I was destined to have a monster year and help my team win the Super Bowl. There was no doubt in my mind we were going to win it all; none.

Our first preseason game was against the Jacksonville Jaguars, and I didn't get one pass thrown my way. I had no catches in the second preseason game, against the Tampa Bay Buccaneers. I had one catch in the third preseason game, versus the Detroit Lions. I had no catches in the fourth preseason game, against the New York Giants. So throughout the entire preseason, I had one catch for seven yards and no touchdowns. That sucked!

I would have understood if it was like last year, when if I didn't get the ball, it was because I hadn't earned it the week before in practice. This time I was having great practices and was very frustrated that the ball wasn't coming to me. I didn't say anything to Tom or the coaches because it was only the preseason. I told myself and believed that if I was open in the games, then when it mattered and Tom needed to make the play, he would throw it to me. I understood that Tom had Wes Welker, Deion Branch, and now Chad Ochocinco to throw to also, but I didn't want to be lost in the shuffle. I just wanted my fair share, and if I got open and made the play, I would deserve it. I wanted only what I would earn. I didn't want the ball because I was his best friend or whatever. I had faith in Tom. Still . . . only one catch for seven yards in four preseason games . . .

I told myself it's all about the season opener against the Miami Dolphins. It was *Monday Night Football* on September 12, 2011, and emotions were high. The game was at Miami and I was hyped. I blocked well, ran great routes, was unselfish, and as I believed, Tom did right by me. I wasn't his go-to guy yet, but I wanted to show Tom that if he threw it to me, he wouldn't regret it. I came through with six tough catches for 86 yards, including a ten-yard touchdown. We won and were off to a good start.

The next week we punished the Chargers. It was a superphysical game and I had four big catches for 86 yards, including two touchdowns. We beat San Diego, 35–21.

We were 2-0 when we went up against my hometown Bills on the road at Buffalo; they were also 2-0. This was for the lead in the AFC East division. I was beyond fired up, the crowd was crazy loud, and the atmosphere was insane. I scored two touchdowns and had seven catches for 109 yards and it should have been my dream come true, but instead it was a nightmare. We had them down 21–0 in the second quarter but let them come back to beat us, 34–31. I was pissed off and it really hurt. After the game my mom told me she never saw me so angry. We were now 2-1 and tied for second place in our division. We had won ten straight regular-season games and now this was a big step back.

We came back to win the next two games and then had our bye week. During my week off, I caught up with a good friend of mine. He introduced me to a girl he was dating. It turned out she was a well-known adult film star. I thought it would be funny to take a private picture of her with my jersey. Next thing I know, it's all over the Internet that I'm hanging out with her and all that. She was my friend's girl, not mine. Nothing happened between us but a picture. It blew up into a big story. When I saw our owner, Mr. Kraft, I apologized to him for causing any embarrassment to the organization. He gave me some great advice, that there will be people out there trying to promote themselves off your name and that you need to be careful about that. I appreciated his advice. The guy is a huge winner with a great family. This one was my fault because it was my idea to take the picture. Live and learn.

After the bye week, we lost the next two games, to the Steelers at Pittsburgh and then home at Foxborough to the Giants. I thought we had the Giants game won when late in the fourth quarter, with 1:36 to go, I scored a fourteen-yard touchdown. I thought wrong. The Giants came right back, and with the help of the referees on a big pass-interference call, they got the ball at the one-yard line for first and goal with thirty seconds left. They scored and beat us. We were now 5-3. The year before we lost only two games the entire season, and now we had three losses only halfway through this one.

We were at a crossroads. I had six touchdowns midway and we had three losses at the eight-game mark—that wasn't Super Bowl caliber. I knew I could do more. I felt ready to explode and take over. The next game against the Jets, I had eight catches for 113 yards and two TDs for a big win on the road, 37–16. Then we had a dominant game against the Chiefs in which I had two crazy touchdowns.

The Chiefs game was a big one for me because I showed I was faster than the defense expected and tough to tackle. I scored on a 52-yard touchdown where Tom threw it to me as I was crossing the middle and then I ran 35 yards down the sideline. The defensive back had the angle on me and hit my legs, thinking I would go down or out of bounds, but I ran through the hit, kept my balance, and raced in for the score. Then on the next touchdown, I caught the ball at the twenty-yard line, broke through the tackle, and knew I was going to get hit low in the knees and out of bounds before I could get to the goal line, so I dove to reach the ball across the goal line. I always wanted to jump in the air and fly across the goal line and it was my best chance to score with the linebacker coming at me. It got crazy when he took my legs out and I flipped over across the goal line, which was pretty cool. I landed on the back of my neck and rolled over. Touchdown! I got up okay and then slammed the ball for my signature Gronk spike.

That was great for my chemistry and my confidence with Tom.

I started to be able to read what he was reading on the field and think what he was thinking. I was anticipating what he was going to do and we were developing a special connection between us. I showed him mad consistency and became his go-to guy.

I now had 10 touchdowns in 10 games, and the all-time touchdown record for a tight end in a single season was 13. We were 7-3 and back on track.

We just kept rolling from there. We beat the Eagles at Philly and I caught my 11th TD. Then we beat the Colts in Foxborough and I scored three more TDs. I thought my third touchdown would be NFL record breaker number 14, but the play was ruled a running play instead of a pass since it was a lateral pitch behind the line, not a forward pass beyond the line of scrimmage. I didn't mind at all. I thought it was cool to have one career carry and score a touchdown, going one-for-one. We were winning at 9-3 and I was happy.

In the next game, I refused to be tackled against the Redskins. It was fun to watch the film in the meetings the next day. I was running over people, through people, and by people. I had 6 catches for a career-high 160 yards and broke the NFL record by scoring two TDs, to set the mark at 15. We were 10-3 with three games to go.

The next two games were come-from-behind wins to beat the Broncos and the Dolphins. They weren't pretty, but we were tough and showed determination to win as a team. When things weren't going our way, we kept fighting, didn't lose faith, and turned it around just in time for the W.

Although I was sharply focused on football, I'm never too busy for my family. It was Christmas time. I had a lot to be thankful for and wanted to get some shopping done for the holiday season. The only thing was, if I went shopping at the mall, I would get mobbed for autographs and would be stuck signing everything for hours and not get any gift shopping done. I told my buddy Dana Parenteau and he had an idea. He offered to get me a costume but the deal was, if he got it, I had to wear it no matter what. I took the deal and he came back with a pair of white sunglasses, a black ZZ Top hat, and a huge fake dark mustache and sideburns. I kept my word, put on a black shirt, pants, and sport coat to match, and went to the mall with Dana. At 6′6″, 260 pounds, sporting a ridiculously huge mustache and sideburns, people stared at me like I was a big creep, but they left me alone so I was okay. Dana and I got all our shopping done and pulled it off!

Now that I had the Christmas shopping out of the way, I was jacked up for the regular-season finale against my hometown Bills. This time we were home at Gillette Stadium. We were now 12-3 and wanted the win to gain home-field advantage through the playoffs as well as even more momentum.

Despite being in our own backyard, we somehow came out flat and were quickly losing 21–0 in the first quarter. This was the same Bills team that gave us our first loss of the season. These were the same Bills who we had had a 21–0 lead against and couldn't stop them from coming back to beat us. Now it was our turn. We weren't going to lose again to these guys and went on to score 49 unanswered points to win 49–21.

That game was very special for me because I was competing

with the Saints' Jimmy Graham for the NFL single-season yardage record for tight end. Jimmy played earlier that day and finished the regular season with 1,310 yards, breaking the previous mark, set in 1980 by Kellen Winslow of the San Diego Chargers. I had already scored two touchdowns to set the NFL record at 17 but I wanted the yardage record, too.

With only 1:30 left in the game and with us up 49–21, I had 86 yards in the game, which had my total at 1,305 yards. I was five yards short of Graham's total. I asked Coach Belichick, Coach O'Brien, and our quarterback Brian Hoyer (Tom was out since we had a huge lead and the game was just about over) to throw it up for a fade route so I could go get it. Both coaches okayed it and Brian, who I had great chemistry with the previous year in training camp, threw me a perfect 22-yarder to break the record and set the mark at 1,327. My 17 touchdowns and 1,327 receiving yards both still stand today and I couldn't have been more proud to score more touchdowns and rack up more yards than any other tight end in NFL history. I appreciated very much that Coach Belichick and Coach O'Brien, who are so team-first oriented, had rewarded me with that last pass. To set those record marks against my Bills made it even sweeter.

The records were cool and all, but I wanted us to win the Super Bowl more than I did anything else. If we had lost that game, the records would have felt hollow, but we won and I felt great.

So now we were 13-3, the top seed in the AFC, and would have home-field advantage in the playoff games leading to the Super Bowl. We had been in a similar situation last year, going into our first playoff game 14-2 and a hot team at home, before suffering a humiliating, bitter loss to the Jets. We had had to live with that all off-season. This was our chance to erase that feeling and we were going to make the most of it.

Tom came out on fire and couldn't miss. He was in the zone, and I got the fever. Tom threw three perfect touchdown passes in the first half to take us up 35–7, and we never let Tim Tebow and the Broncos get back in the game. We won 45–10, and I had 10 catches for 145 yards and 3 TDs. I was knocking tacklers down and they couldn't stop me. I knew we were Super Bowl bound. But to get there, we would have to beat the Baltimore Ravens.

The Ravens were a tough, hard-nosed, physical team. It wasn't pretty and tons of fun like it had been against the Broncos, but we pulled it off and barely got the win, 23–20. What neither I nor anyone else knew at the time was that I had torn my ankle ligament and would need surgery to repair it. It happened in the third quarter and I felt something pop. I was dragging the tackler and my ankle got caught and turned outward underneath him. I knew instantly I was hurt, but I wasn't going to let anything stop me from doing my part to win the game. We had to win this game to get to the Super Bowl, and I wasn't going to sit on the sideline and watch us lose. So after the play I had the trainer tape up the ankle and went back in to finish.

We barely got the win but we were sure thrilled to have it. When the clock ticked down to zero and the game was over, it was one of the happiest moments of my life. I had grown up watching Tom Brady and Coach Belichick in historic Super Bowls. Now

I was a part of a Brady-Belichick Super Bowl team. I was living the dream. It was an unreal feeling.

We would face the New York Giants in Super Bowl XLVI, in Indianapolis. The same Giants who had beaten the Patriots in the Super Bowl four years earlier.

I was so excited in the locker room after the AFC Championship that when a reporter from the ESPN Deportes Channel interviewed me in Spanish and I didn't follow what he was saying, I answered, "Sí . . . yo soy fiesta!"

I meant to say, "I am going to party," and instead I mistakenly said, "I am party." However you say it, and as much as I wanted to party, the reality was I had a big problem. The doctors told Drew and my dad that it would be highly improbable that I would be able to play in the Super Bowl, but I didn't care what they said. I knew I could take any amount of ankle pain for one game. There was no way this was going to stop me from playing in the Super Bowl. This could be my only chance ever! This was my shot to help us win it all and I wasn't going to let everyone down.

I had two weeks to get healthy enough to play in the big game. I spent the first week in a walking boot and wasn't able to practice until the following Thursday, three days before the game. I spent the whole time doing everything I could to strengthen my ankle and recover as much strength in it as I could. It was a terrible break that instead of being superstrong, at my best, like I was right before the injury, I could barely put any pressure on my ankle.

I had been through rehabbing before so I knew the drill. I did all kinds of pool therapy for it and constant ankle exercises. The good news on Thursday was that I was able to jog on it and it didn't hurt unless I tried to accelerate or plant hard on it to cut. I ran routes on air (without someone covering me) and it hurt, but I was encouraged by the progress. I could run and that was good enough for me.

Come game day, I didn't care what percent recovered I was, how explosive I was—whatever. Once you get on the field, you either make the play or you don't—no excuses. Everyone out there has some type of pain they are dealing with and I was no different. We taped up the ankle and it was bulky. It felt funky at first but after a few plays, I got used to it and forgot it was there. This was my dream; this was everything I wanted and worked so hard for. I was so close, only sixty minutes of winning football away.

I had a lot of adrenaline, which got me through the blocking, which I could handle well. Where I struggled was with my explosiveness and change of direction. Through the first three quarters, the game was a low-scoring defensive battle. In the second quarter, I had one catch for 20 yards on a drive that started on our two-yard line and we went all 98 yards for a touchdown and a 10–9 lead. My second target from Tom came at the start of the fourth quarter, at which point we had the lead at 17–15.

It was first and ten at our 43-yard line. I ran a deep route and had a step on the linebacker Chase Blackburn. Tom did an amazing job to escape the pass rush and heave it downfield. The ball was up for grabs. Anytime I have a linebacker covering me one-on-one for a jump ball, I like my chances. I stopped running downfield to jump up for the ball and Chase jumped up for the ball as well. He got it, I didn't. Interception. I had been training my whole life and just had the best regular season of any NFL tight end ever. This guy had been cut and out of work two months ago, in the middle of the season, and yet here he was fifty yards downfield trying to cover me. I was supposed to make that catch. To his credit, Chase out-jumped me and made the play. He is an immortal Giant, a Super Bowl hero. And deservedly so.

As for me, all of my training, my working out, my running, my lifting, my physical therapy to rehab my back, all of it was so that I could make that one play. If I had made that play, we would have been in scoring position and I believe would have won that game. But "if" is for losers and I make no excuses. I got beat in front of the whole world in the biggest game of my life and it was no one's fault but mine. I let my teammates and everyone in my corner down, and it hurt bad.

Chase had intercepted the ball at their nine-yard line and from there we couldn't get anything going offensively. The Giants ended up having the ball with second and goal at our six-yard line with a minute left in the game. Up 17–15, New York could run down the clock and score with no time left. So we let the Giants score from six yards out to give us a chance with a minute left to come back from a 21–17 deficit.

We moved the ball from our 20-yard line to our 49-yard line for the final play. Tom launched a Hail Mary into the end zone. If we catch it, we win, if we don't, well, we lose. The ball came down and bounced off a player toward me. I tried to reach it but it was just out of my grasp. Once again, I had a chance to make the big catch to win the game and couldn't make the play. We lost, and it hurt.

After the game, guys were devastated, some crying, others in shock. All of our hard work, everything we went through for the season, wasn't enough. We came so close only to lose. I kept replaying those two plays in my head over and over again as if I could redo the play and this time catch it. It was very hard to accept. If only I jumped higher on the interception. If only I didn't slow down when the ball bounced off the pile and I kept going, I could have reached it. The hard reality was that the game was over, I didn't make both plays, and I had to accept it. I just wanted to get it out of my mind.

The season was over, but as I walked out of that locker room, I believed without any doubt whatsoever that we would be back for another Super Bowl and have another shot at the greatest sports title in the world.

My family and friends were waiting for me after the game. My ankle hurt and I was miserable about that and how our season had ended. I had two options: go home and cry about it, or go party with my crew. I opted to go party. The Patriots had arranged an after party for the players and bused over those who wanted to go. I went with my dad, brothers, and friends. I got into Party Rocker mode and before long, felt no pain, either mental or physical. I got crazy, which is normal for the Party Rockers. Someone shot video of me with my shirt off, jumping, dancing, chest bumping, and looking wild with my family. It was all over the Internet and I took plenty of criticism for it.

I didn't think it was fair but I don't let haters bother me one bit. The way I saw it, I had had the best regular season any tight end in the history of the NFL ever had. I had worked my butt off and did everything I could to help my team win. We won the AFC Championship and lost a hard-fought game to Eli Manning and the Giants, who played great. My ankle was killing me after playing hurt and I was going to have surgery in a few days, then deal with that rehab hassle. Yeah, we lost, I didn't make the big play on two near misses, and it hurt bad, but I knew I was going to be back and I wanted to deal with it my way, the way that works for me, which is to party with my family and have a good time. With all the hard work I put in that year, I felt I had earned the right to party.

Nevertheless, if it pissed you off, it might make you feel better to know I woke up the next morning with a heck of a hangover.

14

DOWN BUT NOT OUT

didn't know it at the time, but my party rocking after the Super Bowl started off what would later be known as the Summer of Gronk. After having surgery to repair my ankle tear, I spent the off-season having the time of my life. I didn't let the surgery slow me down. First I made sure to get my physical therapy rehab in, then I partied.

With my ankle still in a cast, on February 24, 2012, I spiked, or "Gronked," the ceremonial puck at a Worcester Sharks minor-league hockey game. I obviously couldn't risk injury by walking on the ice, so they drove me out in the back of a shiny new pickup truck. I got out on a small carpet for footing and then Gronked the puck, shattering it. To the roaring crowd, I announced on the mike, "Let's play some hockey!"

I traveled all over the world in March with my brothers and friends. We were going ham and having the time of our lives. You know how the Party Rockers roll!

At the end of the month, I went into a Dunkin' Donuts in Foxborough, put on my jersey, and worked the drive-through for a while. I told the customers we were out of donuts, coffee, and everything else and then said it would be fifty dollars for a croissant-wich. When the customers drove up, I handed them their order and they got a big kick out of it. We all had fun.

After a lot more partying, working out, and fun, I went to Gillette Stadium on June 3 to take part in the Buzz Off for Kids with Cancer. To raise money for pediatric cancer research and to have fun with the kids, I let them shave off all the hair on my head. The event helped raise $500,000 for the cause and I loved hanging out with those kids.

About a week later, after months of negotiations between my agents Drew and Jason with Coach Belichick, we reached an agreement and the Patriots generously extended my contract. Although I had played only two seasons and had two more to go under the current deal, the Patriots ripped it up and gave me a new one. I got a big signing bonus and a huge injury guarantee. With that contract, after only my second year, I became the highest-paid tight end in the history of the NFL! It was a great honor, it was great respect, and it certainly justified my decision in Arizona to turn down the insurance money and go after my dream of being the best tight end to ever play the game. This smart-aleck, troublemaking kid with the constant black eye had made it to the big time.

The key thing for us was that I became the highest-paid tight end and protected myself from injury with guaranteed money. I had talked with my dad, Drew, and Jason for months about this. After going through what I did at Arizona, where my football career was almost taken away from me by injury, we couldn't turn down the financial security of $18 million guaranteed and an average per year of $9 million. Could I have waited another year or two until my rookie contract was up (or longer, if franchised, meaning the Patriots could keep my rights for an additional two years after my deal expired) to get more? Sure, maybe I could have made more money, but I didn't think it was worth it to wait two or more years and risk serious injury for that. There was too much uncertainty. What was certain was that now if my back went out on me again and I could no longer play football, I would get $18 million no matter what. With longtime family friend and financial advisor Fred Rickan in my corner, who has worked with my dad for many years (he was also my Little League coach), I knew I would be financially set. The bottom line was that Mr. Kraft and Coach Belichick did right by me, they believed in me, and I was very happy with our agreement.

The fun train continued with me appearing on the cover of *ESPN The Magazine* totally naked except for a football covering my privates. It wasn't really uncomfortable doing a naked shoot like that, I'm proud of the shape I keep myself in and not embarrassed to share it with the world.

In early July, I appeared on the TV dating show *The Choice* and was matched up with a noncelebrity lady. I had a good time and saw how TV dating shows worked.

On July 10, I went back home to Buffalo and won a celebrity home run contest, which was sweet. The next day, I went to the ESPY Awards in Los Angeles with my dad and brothers and took funny shots of us all on the red carpet.

Well, they say all good things must come to an end, and my Summer of Gronk was no exception. After a nice long break of having fun and getting into great shape, it was time for training camp in Foxborough.

This time around I was coming back to camp a Pro Bowler and NFL record setter. I was no longer looking to prove myself. For me, it was all about having an even better year by doing one thing—winning the Super Bowl. I'd be lying if I said that I was mentally over the two Super Bowl catches I didn't make. No matter how much fun I had, no matter how hard I worked out, nothing could take away the pain, and that's the cost of losing, the consequences of not making the play.

At least in getting the 2012 season started and with the big prize of the next Super Bowl up for grabs in front of us, I could focus on moving forward. There's only one way to get rid of the pain of losing—and that's to win. I knew that I would be forever haunted by those two plays until we won a Super Bowl.

We took care of business in the first regular-season game at Tennessee and beat the Titans, but big problems came my way in week two. We were playing at home against the Arizona Cardinals and in the middle of the game I started feeling back pain. I couldn't believe it. That same pain I felt in my junior year of college from the bad disk was back. I tried playing through the pain but it just got worse. I wanted to get back to the Super Bowl so bad, so I just dealt with the pain, but was miserable. The only thing that kept me going is that we were winning.

By the tenth game of the season, we were 6-3 and playing the Colts at home. I scored two touchdowns that game, which gave me ten so far for the season. I was the first tight end to ever score ten touchdowns in three consecutive seasons, and those were my first three seasons, which made it even more special. My numbers were strong through ten games, with 53 catches for 748 yards. However, I was at my limit. Whatever I did, whether I stood up, sat down, lay down, ran, or did anything else, I couldn't escape the back pain. The stabbing and shooting feelings were getting worse and worse. Then with 3:55 remaining in the fourth quarter of the Colts game, with us up 59–24, I broke my forearm on an extra-point play. It was a freak play. Now I would need surgery to insert a plate and screws in my forearm.

I would be out anywhere from four to eight weeks. My back was hurting so bad that I viewed it as a blessing in disguise. Having those weeks off to rest and rehab my back was huge for me and it worked. I came back after missing five games to play in the final regular-season game, against the Dolphins, and my back felt great. We won, had a 12-4 record, and were headed to the playoffs. My back and forearm felt strong after that Dolphins game; we played great and life was good. The Super Bowl was there for the taking. Now we had to go take care of business in the playoffs, starting with the Houston Texans at home in Foxborough.

In the first quarter of the game, I caught a pass and fell down by the sideline. I landed on the one vulnerable spot, my forearm, in a way that put a ton of weight on it. Despite the plate and screws, I had rebroken my arm. I would need a second surgery to reset my forearm and my season was over. I couldn't believe it. We went on to win the game, and it would have been great if we won the Super Bowl to get rid of the bad feelings from the Giants loss, but the Ravens knocked us out the next week.

I had wanted to play so bad and help us get back to the Super Bowl so much that I probably came back too soon. The team didn't pressure me to come back; they just couldn't stop me from playing once I got the medical clearance to go. It was just bad luck, I guess. It was a terrible feeling to end the season wearing a cast, having a second surgery to the same forearm, and knowing that I was facing the whole off-season again with the same Super Bowl loss still hanging over me.

I reminded myself that we still had a good season, a good core group of players, and we believed we would be back next year to win the Super Bowl. You know me, I do my best to put the past behind me by doing two things—working hard and party rocking hard.

I went to Vegas for Super Bowl weekend and partied with my brothers. We got onstage at a club and were jumping around. I have no explanation as to why but while we were onstage dancing, for no reason other than to get wild, I kicked my brother Gord in the groin and then body-slammed him. Gord takes a beating and keeps on rocking. You gotta love the guy!

I woke up the next morning and saw the video one of my friends sent to me. I was hungover and laughed when I saw it and told him he was crazy for doing that to Gord. He told me to look closely so I could see that it was actually me. Later, as we were walking through the hotel lobby, there on a big screen was video footage of me slamming Gord.

The problem was that I was still wearing a cast on my forearm after my second surgery, and so I took some criticism for not being more careful.

What critics don't understand about me is that it is my inner drive to have fun that makes me able to get up early every morning and do hard work all day long. No one outworks me, and if at the same time it can be said that no one outparties me, then that is just how it's going to be. Look, to this day I still haven't touched one dime of my signing bonus or NFL contract money. I live off my marketing money and haven't blown any big bucks on expensive cars, expensive jewelry, or tattoos. Heck, I still wear my favorite pair of jeans from high school. I spend money on traveling with my family and friends, and on partying, and even then I make sure the tab never gets out of hand. Most of all, I don't hurt anyone (except Gord with the occasional kick to the groin), I don't do drugs, I don't drive drunk, I don't break the law . . . I'm a twenty-three-year-old guy just looking to have a good time. Remember, I don't get crazy during the season; nothing interferes with business, with the goal of success for my team, the New England Patriots. In fact, I think the good times help me stay motivated, stay happy, and generate so much energy to work hard. The truth is, with all the injuries and physical therapy I've gone through, I need to have that balance to keep me going. Partying keeps me positive.

And I needed all the positivity I could get a week later when a doctor told me I had a nasty staph infection in my forearm, most likely from the surgical procedure. I was going to need a third surgery and this was now a career-threatening situation. Your forearm can withstand only so much trauma before the bone becomes unable to heal. Staph infection causes severe and often permanent damage to everything it touches. The third surgery was to take out the hardware that had gotten infected and put new hardware in. At this point I was concerned my forearm would never heal or be able to sustain a hit and my career could be done. I don't get depressed easily but this was kicking a guy when he was already down. Having to walk around with an IV bag filled with antibiotics attached to me for a month sucked.

There was still every reason to believe I could fully heal and come back for the 2013 season, though. Unfortunately, things didn't go well, at all. The crack in my broken bone didn't heal; the break didn't fill in with new bone growth.

To get the crack in my forearm to seal up, I had to have a fourth surgery, in May 2013—a bone graft. This time they took a piece of bone from my hip, processed it into a paste, and put the paste into the crack in my forearm. The idea is that the paste seals up the crack and solidifies the bone. This was now my fourth surgery on my forearm in five months. If I got another staph infection, if the graft didn't seal up the crack and the bone didn't solidify, my career would be over. Either way I would likely miss the first several games of the 2013 season.

I have no funny stories to share about this time of my life, none at all. I went through the fourth surgery and was home all the time. I had to rest my forearm and it drove me nuts. I couldn't do anything fun, couldn't lift, couldn't run, and on top of that, my back pain came back. I was too scared to do anything because a fifth straight forearm surgery would mean the end of my career.

Since I was going to be out four or five months, I decided to go ahead and have my back fixed. Initially I was just going to keep rehabbing it and play through the pain but now that I was going to be out for a while anyway, it made sense to fix my back, too.

So in mid-June 2013, I had my fifth surgery since the previous fall. It was another ruptured disk and Dr. Watkins took care of it for me. He said the disk from the first surgery back in college looked great and that this one should be fine, too. He was right: the pain in my back and legs instantly went away and I felt a lot better.

So now I had to take my time and let the forearm heal up. This was a real low point for me since I was now labeled in the media as injury-prone and kept reading my career was in jeopardy.

One thing I know for sure is that in good times and bad, I can always count on my family. My mom was there for me to help me get through all the surgery, the staph infection, the rehab. After each surgery my mom would make sure I got whatever medication or shots I needed, that my IVs were changed on schedule, and most important, that when I would open the fridge, I could say, "Wow, that's a lot of food." Every time, she had my favorite there for me—her famous chicken soufflé, Rootie's blue cheese, and buffalo wings dip. It's the little things that make all the difference.

With my mom, dad, and brothers behind me, I had all the support I needed to pick myself up and stay positive. When training camp approached in late July 2013, though, I wasn't close to ready to go. My arm had been out of commission for a long time and so it was taking a while to come back. The good news was that all the tests showed that the bone was healing. As I said, my back now felt great, too, so I was getting fired up.

Since I couldn't participate in training camp, I watched practice on the sideline in between my own conditioning drills. I don't like standing around and just watching, so I was always busy, which kept me on track for the fastest-possible recovery. While I was watching a practice, Coach Belichick, who was standing right next to me, turned and said, "Rob, you are one of the hardest workers I've seen and you're always working hard when you're here, but when you're not here . . . I don't know about your craziness off the field, the messing around."

I started laughing and told him, "The fun stuff makes me grind harder, Coach!"

He shook his head as he walked away and said, "Whatever works for you . . ."

He was busting my chops a little, but Coach Belichick gives me the space for me to be me since he knows I always take care of business first. And he knew I was working hard to get ready to play as soon as I could.

But there was no way I could play for the season opener. I had to miss the first six games. Between my dad, Drew, and doctors, and despite how much I wanted to play, they all would have killed me if I didn't wait until week seven. Finally it came. We were 5-1, the team looked good, and I got the green light. The game was on the road against the New York Jets.

Statistically, I had a strong game, leading the team in receiving with 8 catches for 114 yards. In reality, though, I wasn't good enough. My upper body felt really weak. (At this time I was able to bench-press only 225 pounds 7 times. I had done 23 at the NFL Combine and with three more years under my belt I would get close to 30, but right now I was struggling just to get to 7.) I didn't have my conditioning and I was tired. My legs felt slow and heavy since I didn't have them under me yet. I made some good plays during the game and had a huge adrenaline rush because I was so psyched to be playing, but with the game on the line at the end of the fourth quarter, I didn't get things done.

With first and ten at the Jets' 26-yard line and under a minute to go, we were down by three points and needed to score a touchdown to win the game, or kick a field goal to tie and send us to overtime. Tom threw me a pass that should have been the game-winning play. The Jets blitzed and I had to get open across the middle. Tom threw it perfectly and I tried to catch the ball with one hand. I instinctively didn't use my damaged forearm because there was a bulky brace on it and I wasn't used to it yet (it's the same one

I wear now). My arm felt weak and slow, like I was dragging it. My other arm felt quick and strong so I went up to grab the ball with that one, but when I pulled it in to bring it into my other hand the ball somehow got loose and fell away from me. I didn't make the play and we had to settle for a field goal. We went into overtime and ended up losing. Once again I was really disappointed that I didn't make the big play.

By my third game back, I felt good. We had a tough matchup at home against the Steelers and notched a big win, 55–31. I caught 9 balls for 143 yards and a touchdown. This time I felt strong in my upper body and had my legs underneath me. It was great to finally be back in form and feel like myself again.

After a bye week we were 7-2 and getting ready for the Carolina Panthers on *Monday Night Football.* We came up short in a very close game that could have gone either way, but the bottom line is we didn't make enough plays to win. It was a controversial ending where on the last play of the game, Tom threw the ball toward me in the end zone and the linebacker covering me was called for pass interference, which should have given us another down, at the one-yard line, to score with. But the referees reversed the call, saying the ball was not catchable, so there was no penalty and we lost the game. Tom and I disagreed with the call but we Patriots had no choice but to accept it and move on for a huge game against Peyton Manning and the Broncos to see who was the best in the AFC.

We were home but were underdogs for the first time at home in a long time. At the end of the first half we were down 24–0. But we came out in the second half like gangbusters and dominated, to pull off a 34–31 overtime win. It was a great win for us and I felt like we were headed full speed right for the Super Bowl.

We kept that momentum rolling against the Texans. Although we fell behind in the first half, we knew we could come back and get the W, which we did, by the same score as the previous week, 34-31. I finished with 127 yards and a touchdown on 6 catches. We were now 9-3.

Up next we had the Cleveland Browns at Gillette but we came out a little flat. In the middle of the third quarter we were down 12–0 but knew we just needed that big drive to get things going. On first and ten at our 45-yard line, I ran a deep seam route over the middle. I ran right past the linebacker and Tom lofted the ball perfectly right into my outstretched arms. As soon as I caught it and started running, just as I planted my leg, a Browns safety dove full speed right into my knees. I had no chance to defend myself. He took my legs out and I flipped onto my head. The force of that knocked me senseless. I had a concussion and didn't know what was going on, except that my knee was hurt and I couldn't move. Lying there, slowly regaining my wits, I knew my knee was blown out. I knew my season was over . . . again.

I thought of the rehabbing I went through at Arizona and the five surgeries I had just come back from. I had a sick feeling this was finally the end, really the end, that was I done. I was thinking, Is this how it ends for me?

This was the second season in a row that injuries had cut short my season. I would now need a sixth surgery to repair my knee and this time had a bad concussion on top of it all. For me, for who

I am, this was rock bottom. I was knocked down, sprawled out on the canvas, and the ref was counting off ". . . seven, eight, nine . . ."

I was hurt, I was beaten, I was down . . . but not out. Like I was born to do, just like my father taught me to do, like sports had trained me to do, I refused to stay down. I picked myself up off the mat and raised my gloves to keep fighting.

15

GETTING UP

I nstead of celebrating a big win over the Browns and being on top of the world, I found myself lying in the back of an ambulance. My leg had been braced tight so I couldn't move it and we were headed for the hospital so they could check out my head and knee. I had gotten the cobwebs out from the concussion. My dad was sitting next to me on the ride and I could see the concern on his face. I knew I was in real trouble. If people thought I was injury-prone after the five surgeries in thirteen months, what were they going to say now that I needed season-ending knee surgery as well? The bad thoughts kept trying to get deep into my mind that maybe my body just wasn't going to hold up.

I spent the night with a bad headache, dizziness, seeing spots, and nausea. My right knee was swollen like a grapefruit from torn ACL and MCL ligaments. To let the swelling go down and have the best chance of a full recovery, I had to wait a month to have the reconstructive surgery. That was depressing. I looked at myself differently, like I had let everyone down. I went from being super-fast, superbig, superathletic, and superstrong to super-unable to walk. I felt humbled, humiliated, and devastated. I was down and couldn't do anything to prove myself and make up for the Super Bowl loss. This new injury was breaking me and it was getting harder and harder to keep in my heart the belief that I could come back and be the Gronk.

Like I said, I felt like I was at rock bottom . . . that is, until I visited the kids at Boston Children's Hospital with teammate Stevan Ridley, who pushed me around in a wheelchair. It was Christmastime again.

When I visited these sweet young kids who were dealing with real-life adversity and truly fighting for their lives, I was amazed at their strength. I couldn't believe how genuinely happy they were to see Stevan and me. We sang Christmas songs, played board games, and did a lot of other fun activities together. They were so quick to laugh, smile, and have fun that it taught me what heart really is, and what's really important. It meant so much to me to be able to share with them some happiness and fun. I was very emotional, and was blown away by their courage and will to keep fighting, no matter what. I told them to watch me, that I would come back next season and they could root us on to win the Super Bowl.

That day changed everything for me. I realized those kids weren't escaping reality, they were *changing* reality. They were choosing to appreciate the good and fight off the bad. Suddenly my knee surgery seemed like nothing. As I said goodbye to the kids and Stevan wheeled me out, I didn't feel sorry for myself. I felt angry that I had let an injury, not a life-threatening illness or disease, get me down. I wasn't able to get up and walk, but I wanted to get up and fight. These kids showed me what real heart is and I knew I wasn't going to let this latest physical setback break me.

Dr. James Andrews did my knee surgery on January 9, 2014, in Pensacola, Florida. While he was doing the operation, my dad and Drew actually watched it on a big TV monitor visible through the operating room window. I was happy to get that done with.

I did my physical therapy in Miami with Ed Garabedian, who is phenomenal, and my strength and conditioning training with, of course, Pete Bommarito. Drew and I spoke with the Patriots about it first to let them know this wasn't going to be another Summer of Gronk and that they didn't have to worry about me partying in South Beach. The team knew Ed and Pete were top guys and that I would be taking care of business.

I spent a couple of months at a sweet pad in downtown Miami and focused on getting my knee right. With each passing day, just as the strength in my leg came back a little bit more, so did my enthusiastic, playful, and happy personality. During the week I did my work with Ed and Pete. On the weekends I went to a party here and there to reenergize.

In mid-March, my boy Mojo came to visit me. We went to a daytime pool party, which is our favorite kind of fiesta, especially in Miami, where it is summer all year long. You know Mojo was having a good time, party rocking in his Zubaz outfit, dancing nonstop with every girl in the place. I just sat on an outdoor couch and put my leg up. I couldn't dance or move around, but just being around the action picked my spirits up. Sitting at home on the couch doesn't cut it for me.

Jason Rosenhaus showed up to visit for a few minutes and then Mike Katz, my guy at Rosenhaus Sports, kept the party going. Mike is an honorary Party Rocker. While he can't hang and keep up with us the whole night, he's the funniest guy in the world, he's hilarious and crazy—the perfect complement to Drew and Jason for me. Drew is great in dealing with Coach Belichick, Jason has the contract numbers stuff handled for me, and Mike and his brother Jason "J.K." Katz are my designated party guys. Mike fits right in with my Party Rocking crew and J.K. is awesome at getting us into wherever we want to go and making sure we are taken care of.

My fans, even if they didn't realize it, really helped me out that summer. Wherever I went, and even though I was in Miami, my fans were there and gave me mad love. They were so positive I would be back, and so complimentary, that their good energy flowed right into mine.

I did have some fun one afternoon with the Miami-Dade police SWAT team. Mike and Jason Katz set it up for me to go to the firing range and shoot all kinds of cool weaponry. Then I was made an honorary police officer for a day and went on an actual drug bust. I stayed by the truck and watched from outside as the SWAT team kicked in the door and chased down the bad guys. Riding in the truck with ten SWAT guys all armed up and ready for the raid, then seeing them kick in the door, throw smoke grenades, barge in, and take the bad guys down as they tried to flee was extremely cool.

It was like being in an episode of *Cops*. I've got nothing but mad respect for the courage those guys show every day doing their job to protect the neighborhood and keep us safe. To top it off, I went up in a police helicopter with Mike and J.K. That ride was scary!

Aside from a little fun here and there, I got a lot of awesome work done in Miami. Wherever I went, I was disciplined and always had my knee elevated and iced. I lifted weights to get my upper body stronger than it had ever been before. My six-pack was better than ever. Seeing my knee get better and my upper body all jacked got me hyped up.

While waiting on the parking valet guys at my condo one day to go out to dinner, I got impatient and told Mike Katz to shoot a video of me doing push-ups, to show Coach Belichick I was training around the clock. The video showed me in push-up position on the curb. While in push-up position I yelled out, "Yo, Drew, send this to Bill! We're waiting for our car to go out to dinner and look what we're doing! Push-ups at the valet station!" While I beasted out more push-ups, Mike chimed in and said, "Yeah, Bill! You're gonna see a new man!"

I didn't send it to Coach Belichick. I don't think Drew did, either. While I have occasionally texted Tom some video of me party rocking in the middle of the night, I must admit I haven't done that with Coach Belichick . . . yet!

The bottom line was that when I stepped onto that plane in Miami, bound once again for Boston, it was goodbye to that injury-plagued year. I put it all behind me. Now it was time to step back into the ring and start my 2014 season. I had fallen hard in 2013; in fact, I fell so hard that I got a concussion. Since then, every fan I had seen, and especially all the kids, had told me that I would be back. That I could do it. The moment we touched down at Logan Airport, I knew with everything I had that it was time to prove them right.

16

THROWING HAYMAKERS

I knew when I walked in the door at Foxborough for the start of team workouts in April 2014 that Coach Belichick would kick my butt if I wasn't in good shape or was behind schedule on my rehab. I did not want to get reamed out. So I didn't just show up in good shape—I showed up in *great* shape and ahead of my rehab schedule. Just as important, the Gronk showed up, period. I was back! The real me, not the one who couldn't stand up.

I wasn't able to run yet, but I looked like Gronk, talked like Gronk, and let everyone know that I would soon be playing like Gronk. Thank God, the next month in May I could start jogging very lightly, and was able to make progress through July and into training camp.

But before I started training camp in late July, there was something I had to do, something very important to me. I had to visit my friends at Boston Children's Hospital again. The last time I had been there, I was in a wheelchair, and although I had gone to cheer them up, it was the kids who totally cheered *me* up. There's no one more likable than these courageous kids who fight with so much strength of heart despite being really sick. It means a lot to me to help them. I walked around that hospital this time and loved lifting their spirits.

Earlier that day, and as I had done every year since the Summers of Gronk began, I participated in the One Mission Buzz Off for Kids with Cancer, held at Gillette Stadium. It's a great charitable event where the kids get to shave my head and others'. As much as anything in my career, I'm superproud that I have helped these folks raise money for pediatric cancer research, including more than $1 million in 2014. Pardon the promo, but please come to the next event and register at buzzforkids.org, and for other Gronk Nation events, which you can check out at gronknation .com. My dad established the Gronk Nation Youth Foundation for me, my dad, Gord, Dan, Chris, and Glenn to all give back to the community and to help those who can use it. The Gronk Nation Youth Foundation has an annual Gronkowski football camp, gets involved in the Boston Marathon, and participates in or sponsors other great events.

At training camp in August, my quad and hamstring muscles were getting stronger. I ran routes on air and was able to run full speed and cut. I focused on building endurance in my knee. I was careful, doing a little more each time so that my knee could handle the workout without swelling up and then being too sore the next day. At the beginning of camp, my knee could handle only a few minutes of hard route running. By the end of the preseason, right before the season opener against the Miami Dolphins, I was ready to test my knee and practice.

Here's how the practice schedule typically works before a game. On Monday, we have a light day of watching film from the game the day before, and we go to the training room to get treatment on our injuries from the game. Tuesday is an off day unless you have to come in for treatment. Wednesday is the big offensive day of full-pad practice where we install the key plays we expect to use during the game. Thursday is another important day of practice, where you work on third down and other special plays. Friday is a light day in shorts where we review the plays from Wednesday and Thursday and work on red zone plays. Saturday is typically either travel or another superlight day. Sunday is game day.

On the Wednesday and Thursday practices, I was able to practice well enough to get the green light for the season opener against the Dolphins, at Miami. I was expecting to step onto the field and automatically have that magical connection with Tom and be at All-Pro form. I was wrong. Tom threw 11 passes my way and I caught only 4 of them. One of them was a six-yard touchdown in the second quarter to put us up 17–7. The best part of the game for me was not the catch, but Tom getting crazy celebrating the touchdown by head-butting me and then smacking my face mask around. He was fired up and I loved it. I wanted us to get hot and keep the momentum going but we just got cold from there. It all fell apart as we gave up 21 unanswered points in the second half to lose 33–20. I just couldn't get anything going in that second half and we lost our opener. Being 0-1 was terrible.

As much as I wanted to run explosive routes and block strong, I didn't have the strength or conditioning yet. My timing was off with my routes and I wasn't getting separation. I played about a third of the snaps against the Dolphins and just couldn't contribute the way I wanted to. After the game, my knee swelled up like a grapefruit. I had to stay off my knee and ice it down for the next couple of days. I couldn't practice on Wednesday, the big day of offensive practice, where as I said you install all the plays and run them to get them down and have good chemistry. Without that work I can't get my timing down with Tom, either.

Because of that, I had less play time in the next game, in Minnesota against the Vikings, and didn't have a big role. We won and so we went to 1-1, which was good, but my knee still wasn't right. I didn't feel like myself and was fighting through it, trying to get my groove back. In week three, against the Oakland Raiders in Foxborough, I caught a six-yard touchdown pass in the second quarter, but I was still having a tough time feeling fast, explosive, or strong. The bottom line, though, is that we won the game, 16–9, to get us to 2-1, so I was staying positive.

Next up was *Monday Night Football* at Kansas City. I had a much better week of practice going into this game. The swelling in my knee was going down and I was fired up for this to be my breakout game. I was ready to show everybody I was back and take over! Once again, it didn't happen the way I envisioned. It was all Chiefs all night long. They were dominant and our offense couldn't get anything going. I had only two targets from Tom and caught one of them. When Tom threw an interception for a touchdown in the middle of the fourth quarter and it was 41–17, Coach Belichick took Tom out of the game. Brady was getting sacked and getting hit. I wasn't being much help to him and there was no point of Tom staying in and risking injury with the game out of hand. Our backup quarterback Jimmy Garoppolo came in on the next drive and I scored a thirteen-yard touchdown that was by far my best play of the season to that point.

I played superhard on that play because I was mad we were being humiliated on *Monday Night Football*. We were too far behind to come back and everyone knew it was over, but I went hard with everything I had. I refused to be tackled and powered through four defenders to fight my way into the end zone for what looked like a meaningless touchdown. But it wasn't meaningless to me. I was fighting to get back to being the Gronk who breaks tackles and scores touchdowns.

After the game, I heard that a reporter asked Coach Belichick whether the quarterback situation would be evaluated. Coach looked at him like he was the dumbest idiot in the world, rolled his eyes, and gave a little rhetorical laugh to scoff at the question. Coach knew what we knew, which is that Tom Brady is the best quarterback, ever. No disrespect to the other great ones, but that's how I see it. Period. When a lot of people in the media and the public had doubts about Tom's ability, Coach Belichick never for one second turned on Tom. Coach showed total faith in him. We all felt that way. We knew how hard Tom was working, how much he was preparing, how competitive he was and wanted to win.

If anyone wasn't playing up to par and was letting the team down, it was me. I was still not playing all the downs, I was coming in and out, not practicing to the max, and I felt I was hurting the flow of our offense. I needed to do more. I needed to step up. I wanted to come through for Tom, for all of my teammates and coaches, and for all the Patriots fans. We were now 2-2 and at a crossroads.

Although the game was a bitter, high-profile loss on *Monday Night Football,* I didn't come away from the game pessimistic at all. In fact, I came away completely *optimistic.* Just like in my rookie year when I made the big mistakes against the Browns that cost us the game, I had also made some really good plays that night and took that positive momentum into a great week of practice.

The timing of the Chiefs loss was perfect because our next game was on *Sunday Night Football,* at home against the Bengals. Coach Belichick said it best after the Chiefs game: "On to Cincinnati." The only way I can get over a bad loss is to come back with a big win. This would be a big Sunday night matchup.

I was excited because my knee did not swell up or interfere with my Wednesday practice and I was able to have a really good week. I have no doubt everyone on that team believed the Chiefs game had been a fluke. We all knew that if we supported each other, came together, didn't point fingers, and held ourselves accountable for our own assignments, we could turn this around.

Going into the Sunday night game, my confidence was high and I felt ready to play my kind of football. I told my brother Chris right before the game that I was going to help make No. 12 look like Tom Brady again.

My first pass came in the first quarter and was a 27-yard play. With that pass, Tom became the sixth player in NFL history to throw for more than 50,000 yards. The crowd cheered when the announcer congratulated Tom on the play, but Tom was much happier on the next play when he threw a touchdown to put us up 14–0. Tom Brady is all about winning and putting the team first, before any individual accomplishments. He sets the ultimate example for us all.

From there Tom took the game over and was dominant. And I was back! I had 6 catches for 100 yards and scored a sixteen-yard touchdown in the third quarter to put us up 27–10. We just kept rolling from there and it was a great win for Tom, for Coach Belichick, for all of us. I played a lot and was very happy with all phases of my game. There had been a lot of criticism in the week leading up to Cincinnati that all the injuries had taken their toll on me, that I wasn't going to make it all the way back. But this game was a statement that Tom Brady was back, Rob Gronkowski was back, and the whole New England Patriots were going to be a contender this season.

What to me was most important about that game, other than the win, of course, was that I had played without fear. The first couple of games, I was not confident in my knee. That lack of confidence hurt my speed and strength. It was one big vicious cycle. The only way to run full speed, to give everything to make the catch and run through tackles, is to be fearless. I have to play that way or not at all. When I'm in the zone, I don't worry about injuries. I feel like I've had my share of them in the past and now they're behind me. I am one hundred percent focused on going for the big play.

I need to be that way because every week when I play, when I look across the line at the defender, I can see in his eyes that *he* is ready for *me*. I know he prepared for me all week because he doesn't want to lose and get embarrassed. So everyone I go against brings their A-game against me and I love it. To me that is respect and it only heightens my focus and intensity.

From there, we beat the Bills at Buffalo; it's always a special game for me, playing against my hometown team. Then we had a Thursday night game against the Jets, whose defense, then still under Coach Rex Ryan, always plays us supertough. Thursday night games are brutal because four days is not enough time to recover from the Sunday game previous. You could tell everyone was beat up and it was a very tough, physical battle to the end. But we outfought the Jets 27–25 and played well under the circumstances.

The only good thing about a Thursday night game is that you then get extra days to recover before the next matchup, in this case the Chicago Bears at Gillette Stadium on Sunday, October 26. Tom and I made the most of the extra time in practice. We worked on this red zone play where I am supposed to run a short route toward the corner of the end zone.

In the first quarter of the Bears game Tom called the play at the six-yard line. It was smoother in practice, but Tom made the perfect throw and I dove to catch the ball and just got my feet down. I didn't have to dive in practice but it's always tougher in the game. In the next quarter, we had a similar play and Tom put the ball in a great spot, knowing exactly where I could reach it, grab it in, and get my feet down for the touchdown. The defender had excellent coverage but the throw was perfect, so he couldn't stop it. And in the third quarter, with the ball at the Bears' 46-yard line, Tom threw it to me and I caught it around the 35-yard line. I refused to go down: I threw the defender off me and raced toward the goal line, dragging another defender along for the ride five yards and into the end zone. That was my third score, a hat trick! We won big, 51–23, and went to 6-2. I had 9 catches for 146 yards, with three touchdowns. I was excited because I had made nine catches out of nine targets. I really came through for Tom. It was on the last touchdown that I knew I was back all the way, because from start to finish I felt dominant that play. At this point my knee was an afterthought; I didn't even ice it after the game.

Now we had Peyton Manning and the Broncos at home. They were considered to be the best team in the AFC and this game would put that idea to the test. Knowing what was on the line, we had a really good week of practice as a team; we were focused and everyone was ready. Denver got off to a 7–3 lead in the first quarter, but after that we took over. We scored 24 points in the second quarter and never let up, winning convincingly, 43–21. I had two really positive plays in the fourth quarter, one of them a touchdown to put the game out of reach. That was my fiftieth career touchdown, which was nice, but all I cared about was that we won and were now 7-2. Plus we had a bye week ahead, which was a great time for me to rest up. My body was tired and needed a break. I spent the weekend at Dallas. I flew there with my brothers to watch Goose play for Kansas State against TCU.

At this point, every game was a big game. We had a playoff mentality and were extremely intense in practice. Our next tough assignment was to go to Indianapolis and take on the Colts. Our offensive coordinator, Josh McDaniels, called a great game and we executed the plays very well. Jonas Gray ran the ball 37 times for 201 yards and scored four touchdowns, an awesome performance. I blocked and blocked and blocked some more and loved it. Our offensive line was dominant.

I was loving it until one of the Colts' defenders was talking trash, so on first and goal, at the snap, I grabbed him and drove him back toward the sideline and beyond, and he landed on his butt five yards out of bounds. Meanwhile Jonas ran the ball in for one of his touchdowns. After the game, I told Cris Collinsworth of NBC that I took the guy and "threw him out of the club" like a fed-up bouncer on that touchdown play.

On our next offensive series, on third and four at Indy's 26-yard line, Tom threw me a short pass by the sideline. I spun and got the linebacker off me at the twenty-yard line and then cut toward the middle of the field to run through two tackles (with Julian Edelman's awesome block), then raced toward the end zone and drove through two more tacklers at the goal line. NBC's Al Michaels said

I ran like a runaway truck on that one. This one play proved that my speed, explosiveness, and power were better than ever. I wasn't just back, I was at my best. After the play, I went to the sideline and had some fun dancing. Between kicking the guy out of the club, the sweet touchdown run, and my smooth dance moves on the sideline, I guess I contributed my share of highlights for a game that had plenty of them. The bye-week rest did me a lot of good and it showed.

We faced a tough Detroit team the following week at Gillette but we all played well as a team and won 34–9. Now at 9-2, we had a big-time matchup against the Packers at Green Bay. A lot of experts said we were the two best teams. Going to Green Bay is the ultimate test because the atmosphere at Lambeau Field is like no other. We played well but lost 26–21 in a very close game that we could have won. While I had 7 catches for 98 yards, I dropped one that would have won the game for us. Late in the fourth quarter, we had the ball at the Green Bay twenty-yard line. We were still down 26–21. We called a play for me to run down the sideline and make the catch in the end zone. I did catch the ball but as soon as I did, the safety made an excellent play to knock the pigskin out of my hands.

I had let the team down in a huge game. After the play, I went to the sideline and told my tight end coach that I wanted us to run that play again, and that the next time we did, whenever that was, I was going to catch it. That play stayed with me and wasn't going to let me be until I could make things right. Meanwhile, after Green Bay there was nothing I could do but get ready with my teammates for the next game, at San Diego. We flew straight to Southern California for the week.

We were ready for San Diego and they were ready for us. They played well and fought hard but we made more plays to win the game and go to 10-3. I had 8 catches for 87 yards and scored a 14-yard touchdown, which was my tenth touchdown of the year. It was my fourth season of ten or more touchdowns, which tied me with the Chargers' own Antonio Gates for the record. Again, the records are nice but for me it's all about the Super Bowl.

Now we had Miami at home, the same team that had beaten us in the season opener. The first half was slow going for us and I didn't have any catches, but on the first play in the second half, I caught a nice pass down the middle for 34 yards and we exploded from there to score 24 points in the second quarter. We won 41–13 and were a very different team from the team that lost in the opener. In the first game we fell apart in the second half. In this game we dominated the second half. We wanted payback against them for that first loss and we got it. Instead of me playing a third of the downs, I played all of the downs until the game was out of reach. I had 3 catches for 96 yards, including a 27-yard touchdown.

We were 11-3 with two games left to close out the regular season, both against AFC East rivals who always play us tough. First we had to go on the road to play the Jets. Their season was toast and it looked like Rex Ryan was going to be fired the minute it was over. They had nothing to lose, but like I said earlier, Rex gets his defense to show up and play tough and smart. This was an all-out battle and the Jet players brought it for Rex. Meanwhile, this was a must-win game for us. We could gain home-field advantage throughout the playoffs and a first-round bye.

I drew first blood with a touchdown in the first quarter but the Jets took the lead and held it throughout the third quarter, 13–10. We were able to punch in a one-yard run to retake the lead, and from there our defense kept the Jets in check.

Since we had home-field advantage throughout the playoffs, we had nothing to play for in the last week of the regular season, at home against the Bills, so the starters didn't play much, if at all. We lost but it didn't matter. My body felt run-down and needed the rest. I would now have two weeks to get ready for our first playoff game, against the Ravens.

My stats for the regular season through the 15 games I played in were 82 catches, 1,124 yards, and 12 touchdowns. I made the Pro Bowl and at that point in my career had set a lot of NFL records: youngest player with 3 TD receptions in a game (2010, rookie year at twenty-one years old); youngest player with 3 TD receptions in a playoff game (2011, at age twenty-two); most TD receptions by a tight end in a season, 17 (2011); most TDs by a tight end in a season, 18 (2011); first tight end to lead the NFL in receiving TDs (2011); most receiving yards by a tight end in a season, 1,327 (2011); most offensive TDs in first two seasons, 28 (tied with Randy Moss); most seasons with 10+ TDs by a tight end, 4 (2010–2012, 2014 tied with Antonio Gates); and most consecutive seasons with 10+ TDs by a tight end, 3 (2010–2012).

Ever since I was a kid, I had wanted to set records like that.

I wanted to be the best ever. Now what I wanted more than anything was to be a Super Bowl champion. I wanted that ring more than any of those records. The pain of the Super Bowl loss, of not making the big plays when I needed to—those things made the NFL records less important to me. What I wanted was three games away.

Round one was an up-and-down battle. The Ravens went up 14–0 against us in the first quarter. We rallied back to tie it up in the second but by the third quarter we were down again, 28–14. Needing the score to bring us within seven points, we were at the Ravens' five-yard line. Tom and I had practiced a quick slant route all week long and when he called that play now, I was excited. I knew Tom was going to come to me. After the snap I ran a good route to get inside and Tom fired it right in there for a touchdown. From there we went on to win, 35–31.

We had been down before and came back all throughout the season. We knew that if we kept working, we were going to come back. And the key thing is, when we were down we didn't point fingers and blame each other. When the heat was on, we stayed cool and stayed together.

Now we had to win one more, the AFC Championship game, to get to the Super Bowl. The Indianapolis Colts stood in our way, but in that game we ended up dominating them on both sides of the ball. Just like the last time, we ran the ball down their throats. It didn't matter to us if we won throwing it or running it. We just wanted to win, and when the clock ticked down and the scoreboard showed a final score of 45–7, it was Super Bowl XLIX in Glendale, Arizona, here we come!

Realizing that I was going to the Super Bowl, that I would get my chance to make everything right, to win it all, was almost painfully exciting. I knew I had a long two-week wait before the game. I didn't get too excited, because unless you *win* the big game, you lose. So the next two weeks was all about having good practices and doing everything I could to prepare for the NFC champion Seattle Seahawks. I knew Seattle's defense was as good as any I had ever faced and that as defending Super Bowl champs, they were going to give us their best.

The first offensive play of the game was a short two-yard pass to me. I got dropped as soon as I caught it. Seattle's defense was smart, athletic, fast, and hard-hitting. That first play set the tempo of their defense. They stopped us on that drive and we punted. On the next drive, we got the ball to midfield on third and three. Tom fired in a short quick pass to me for four yards and a first down. We kept the drive going but turned it over deep in their territory.

Both teams were scoreless in the first quarter but that changed in a big way in the second. With just 36 seconds left in the half, the score tied at 7–7, and the ball at the Seattle 22-yard line, Tom called the play—the same play I didn't make in the Packer game. We had worked on that play all week during practice for Seattle. I was ready.

As I lined up wide toward the sideline, I didn't want to think of anything. I knew Tom was going to throw the ball to me. For what was only a second but seemed like an eternity, I saw myself get boxed out on the deep ball in the Giants game in Indianapolis. I saw the ball fall just out of my reach on the Hail Mary. This would now be my chance. My time to shine. This was my shot to score a touchdown in the Super Bowl and help us win it all. This would be the biggest play in the biggest game of my life. Then I emptied all these thoughts from my mind.

I knew what I had to do. I had to make a move at the line and then run by the linebacker. When Tom snapped the ball, I did exactly what I was trained to do. I got open and raced down the sideline with everything I had. Tom threw the most perfect pass ever. As I watched the ball come right to me in full stride, I reached up with both hands to grab it. I wasn't thinking anything. I was focused and looked that ball in and then when I got it, held it tight with both hands. The linebacker tried to knock it out but nothing was going to break this ball from my grip. We went down in the back of the end zone and I jumped up and Gronked that ball. YESSSSSSSS!

This time, I made the play. This time, nothing but sheer happiness. After Gronking it, I held my fist in the air, knowing that I did it. My teammates mobbed me and it was a great moment, no doubt, but I knew there was a whole half left to go. I knew that if I didn't make more plays, if I didn't block my best and do everything I could to help us win, the hurt of losing would still be there.

We all knew that Pete Carroll, Marshawn "Beast Mode" Lynch, and the rest of the Seahawks weren't going to lie down and die.

This was going to be a heavyweight fight that went the distance. And sure enough, with six minutes left to go in the fourth quarter, we were down by three points. We had to move the ball down the field and get some points if we were going to have a chance to win. It was make-it-or-break-it time. Tom completed nine out of nine passes in a row on that drive. On second and eleven at our 48-yard line, I caught a twenty-yard pass to put us in field goal range. Two plays later I caught a thirteen-yard pass that got us into the red zone. From there Tom hit Julian Edelman for an incredible touchdown that put us up 28–24 with about two minutes to go.

Praying that our defense would hold up and win the game, I watched helplessly as the Seahawks marched down the field. On the craziest play, Seahawks receiver Jermaine Kearse, lying on his back, managed to pull in a ball that was still bouncing and floating around above him after he had initially failed to catch it. I couldn't believe our bad luck. It was an impossible catch and now they had the ball at our five-yard line with only a minute to go.

I thought back to the Giants game where in the same situation, our defense decided to let New York's Ahmad Bradshaw run the ball in for a score so there would be some time left on the clock for us to get the ball back. Coach Belichick didn't do that this time. Instead we tackled Marshawn at the one-yard line. I thought for sure that with only twenty-six seconds left the Seahawks would run it again. I hoped our defense could stop them again. In what would become the happiest moment of my life, I watched our cornerback Malcom Butler do exactly that as he shot in front of the receiver to intercept the ball.

In shock and in complete elation, we went nuts on the sideline. I realized at that moment that we were going to win the Super Bowl. A wave of goose bumps, chills, and emotion washed over me and swept away all the pain. The four surgeries on my forearm, the terrible infection that wouldn't let my arm heal, the IV bag of antibiotics attached to me that I had to walk around with for a month, the long hours of rehab, all the hard work, not making the big plays against the Giants, losing the Super Bowl, the disappointment of two season-ending injuries ever since, the talk that I couldn't make it back from the injuries, that all left me. It was pure happiness. I couldn't think about anything, I could only feel the dream that I wanted more than anything in the world. I did it! We did it together! YESSSSSSSS!!!!!!!!!!

Since there was still twenty seconds left, we had to take the field and snap the ball. When Tom took a knee, the emotions of two hard-fighting teams took over and a brawl erupted. It was understandable. This was a brutal loss and tough to accept with the stakes so high. When it happened, someone hit me, so I hit someone back. Yes, I threw some haymakers; it was all in good fun. I wouldn't have it any other way.

After the game, I danced in the middle of the field with my teammates, savoring the moment. Standing up onstage, holding up the Vince Lombardi Trophy in victory was unreal. That was the ultimate.

From there it's been a nonstop party with the city of Boston. We had an awesome victory parade where fans threw jerseys for me to sign, footballs, even cans of beer for me to chug. It was a blast!

I did another epic Gronk puck spike, this time when the Boston Bruins and their fans honored us before a game in TD Garden a few days after the Super Bowl. I won the Comeback Player of the Year Award, and that was special to me, but it's the Super Bowl ring on my finger that shines brightest.

After a few months, the feeling of winning it all goes away, which makes you want it back. The 2015 season is getting closer as I write this. What now? Well, I can promise you three things. One, I'm going to party rock. Two, I'm going keep Gronking that football. And three, no matter what, I will always be me, always be Gronk!

ACKNOWLEDGMENTS

To my mom, Diane, first off, you are the greatest mom in the world! How you put up with all five of us, especially me, is amazing. You have always been there for me, especially during the surgeries. First, thank you for always making our meals every day and never showing up with fast food or frozen dinners. You're truly awesome! Second, thanks for always taking me to my sporting events, to activities, and for helping me with my homework all the time. Third, thanks for giving me all those whuppings with that hard plastic spoon. You beat me up so much that these NFL tackles don't hurt! I really love you and am very proud that we are closer now than we have ever been.

To my dad, Gordy, you are the ultimate Papa Gronk! No dad

commands more respect from his sons than you. Thank you for helping me grow into the man I am today and for introducing me to the world of athletics. You taught me how to work hard, how to get better, to listen to my coaches, and what it takes to go to the next level. Thanks for being at all of our sporting events, for coaching us, and for teaching us how to enjoy life to the max and party rock! You're one supercool guy!

To my brothers, who are my best friends and the best brothers I could ever ask for. Each of you made me into the competitive, hard-nosed, fearless NFL player I am today. Gord, Dan, Chris, and Goose—thank you for toughening me up.

To my late great-grandfather Ignatius Gronkowski, for starting the tradition of athletic excellence in our family as a member of the 1924 U.S. Olympic cycling team in Paris.

To my grandpa Tom Weber and grandma Carol Weber for hosting us all the time at the lake house when we were kids. Thanks for the fun times.

I want to thank my high school coaches Mike Mammoliti, George Novak, Bill Gorman, Chuck Swierski, and Harry Shaughnessy. My trainers Demeris Johnson, Randy Cohen, and Pete Bommarito. My physical therapist, Ed Garabedian. My college coaches Mike Stoops and Dana Dimel.

I want to thank my main man, #12, Tom Brady. Thank you for being a real drill sergeant and believing in me. I also want to thank my head coach, Bill Belichick; the Patriots' owner, Mr. Robert Kraft; and coaches Josh McDaniels, Brian Daboll, Bill O'Brien,

Brian Ferentz, and George Godsey. I also want to thank the New England Patriots' head trainer, Jim Whalen, and the training staff.

My financial advisor, Fred Rickan, who has been a longtime family friend and great financial guru for me and my family.

I would like to thank Derek Jeter—I am proud to be a part of your publishing team.

I would like to thank Bari Wolfman for her help with this project from start to finish.

My agents at Rosenhaus Sports, starting with Drew Rosenhaus, the leader of the team, Jason Rosenhaus, Mike Katz, Jason Katz, Robert Bailey, LeRon McCoy, and Kathy Picard. Thanks for negotiating my awesome contract and for leading me in the right direction.

Jason Rosenhaus, my coauthor, thanks for taking the time from your work and family to help me out with this book of my life experiences, from when I was a kid to winning the Super Bowl. You did a great job of explaining the story, getting into detail, and making it real-life intense for the reader to enjoy. You've got mad and extraordinary writing skills!

JASON

To my daughter, Aubrey: When I first started my courtship with your mother, she showed me a picture of herself as a cute little eight-year-old girl. I liked the picture but decorated my office instead with the pictures of your mother from when she was a Miami Dolphin cheerleader, a Miami Heat dancer, a fitness model, etc. . . .

Then one day, everything about my life was turned upside down when I learned I was going to have a daughter. Suddenly I thought of that picture of your mother as a little girl, the one I put away in my desk. The first chance I got, I put the picture of that smiling little girl right next to my computer screen so I could look at it all the time. I saw a little girl who had her birth mother and father taken away from her. I wanted to be there to help her through it, to make everything okay, but I couldn't. That was the past. You would now be my future and no matter what, I was going to be there for you. I looked at that picture every day and imagined how wonderful it would be to have a daughter just like the one in the picture. You see, I grew up always thinking I would have sons, and that was how I expected my life to be. And then just like that, when you came into our lives, you were such a cute, sweet baby, with such a gentle, vulnerable look in your eyes; I would never be the same.

From that moment on, I wanted to protect you from the world, to keep you safe and happy. And now that you are eight years old, I want to hang on to your youth where your daddy is the man of your life, but I know that won't last. I know when you get older, you will make the most important decision of your life, which is choosing the man you will marry. Much to my chagrin, I can't make that decision for you, but with your mom as the perfect role model, we can raise you to be a good decision maker. Because of you, I want to be the type of husband to your mother that you will want for yourself. You make me demand of myself that I set the right example of the type of man and husband I would want for you. You motivate me to work hard, to be my best, to never quit, and to do what's right. I know this . . . because you have that special quality to inspire me, the same as your mother. I'm so proud of who you are becoming. Most of all, you will always be that sweet little baby girl to me, filling my heart with unconditional love, which is how you win in life, and I thank you for that.

To Gronk, thanks for teaching this forty-five-year-old NFL agent and father of three that it's a good thing to dance like a Party Rocker without a care in the world and enjoy the moment. From the first time I met you in 2009 through today, where you have become a true NFL superstar, I have been astounded at how you haven't changed and have stayed remarkably humble and fun-loving.

A special thank-you to Gordy for having the confidence in me to get the job done in such a short period of time and to do it right! The way you look after *all* of your sons, the example that you set, the discipline you have instilled within them, and the smart guidance you provide are truly remarkable. There is no higher compliment than your faith in Drew and me to represent Dan, Chris, and Rob as their agents.

I want to thank my partner and brother, Drew, who carries the weight of our one hundred combined clients on his back and can still beat most of them in a three-mile race! As always, our clients can count on you to come through for them, and I appreciate your having held down the fort while I worked after-hours on this assignment. Like Gronk, you are fearless and overcome all adversity to win.

I also want to thank Robert Bailey for nominating me for the job of coauthoring this book. Mike and Jason ("J.K.") Katz deserve special mention for taking great care of the Gronks. To Robert, Mike, J.K., and the rest of the RSR team—LeRon McCoy, Ryan Matha, Kevin Highmark, and especially Howard Rosenhaus—thanks for always having my back and taking the fight to the competition.

I want to thank my office manager, Kathy Picard, for her 100 percent loyalty, reliability, and research on this assignment.

For making this book happen, I would like to thank Derek Jeter and the whole team at Gallery Books: Louise Burke, Jennifer Bergstrom, Jeremie Ruby-Strauss, Nina Cordes, Jennifer Robinson. Also Ian Kleinert—the best literary agent in the business.

To my parents, Robert and Jill, thank you for giving Drew, me, and my sister, Dana, a wonderful childhood, great direction, and for always putting your children first.

Last but not least is my amazing wife, Cassandra Hall, who makes my life a dream come true with her kindness, unselfishness, and love. It hasn't been super-easy to put up with me while I worked overtime on this, but your patience and support helped me keep at it. I could not have pulled this off without having complete trust and confidence in you as my wife and mother of Aubrey, Bronson, and Colton. As for Bronson, thank you for making coming home to your excited cheer the best part of my day. And to little Colton, the one-year-old, rugged mama's boy of the group, you are the sparkle in your mother's smiling eyes!